Learning SQLite for iOS

Extend SQLite with mobile development skills to build great apps for iOS devices

Gene Da Rocha, MSc, BSc (Hons)

[PACKT]
PUBLISHING

open source*
community experience distilled

BIRMINGHAM - MUMBAI

Learning SQLite for iOS

First published: March 2016

Production reference: 1180316

Published by Packt Publishing Ltd.
Livery Place
35 Livery Street
Birmingham B3 2PB, UK.

ISBN 978-1-78528-897-5

www.packtpub.com

Credits

Author
Gene Da Rocha, MSc, BSc (Hons)

Reviewer
Alvaro Franco

Ting Xiao

Acquisition Editors
Larissa Pinto

Subho Gupta

Content Development Editor
Rashmi Suvarna

Technical Editor
Anushree Arun Tendulkar

Copy Editors
Charlotte Carneiro

Yesha Gangani

Ameesha Green

Project Coordinator
Judie Jose

Proofreader
Safis Editing

Indexer
Tejal Daruwale Soni

Graphics
Abhinash Sahu

Production Coordinator
Aparna Bhagat

Cover Work
Aparna Bhagat

About the Author

Gene Da Rocha, MSc, BSc (Hons) in mobile and computer science is an experienced IT professional with over 25 years in the IT industry. He has worked for a variety of companies nationally and internationally, in different industries including corporate, start-up, pharmaceutical, finance, banking, and the NHS.

Gene is also the owner and founder of a mobile solutions company, Voxstar (www.voxstar.com), based in London and Buckinghamshire. He comes from a programming and development background, and has worked with database technology, iOS, Android, Windows mobile, and a variety of other technologies.

He has been helping and advising, programming, and recently testing software for a number of companies such as DigitasLBI, Oxfam, News UK, QAWorks, Reuters, and the Association for Project Management, among many others.

About the Reviewer

Alvaro Franco is an iOS engineer and web developer. He has contributed to the iOS and OS X open source community. He has also been a part of Aluana, building Mindrop, and companies such as Mozilla, where he contributed to delivering Firefox for iOS. Alvaro is also a motorsport fan and guitarist.

Ting Xiao, is a frontend developer focusing on how to make things good on the webpage; she is also working on the development of a mobile app simultaneously. She is interested in any brain technology. According to Ting, thanks to the technology, we can know this world much better.

www.PacktPub.com

eBooks, discount offers, and more

Did you know that Packt offers eBook versions of every book published, with PDF and ePub files available? You can upgrade to the eBook version at www.PacktPub.com and as a print book customer, you are entitled to a discount on the eBook copy. Get in touch with us at customercare@packtpub.com for more details.

At www.PacktPub.com, you can also read a collection of free technical articles, sign up for a range of free newsletters and receive exclusive discounts and offers on Packt books and eBooks.

https://www2.packtpub.com/books/subscription/packtlib

Do you need instant solutions to your IT questions? PacktLib is Packt's online digital book library. Here, you can search, access, and read Packt's entire library of books.

Why subscribe?

- Fully searchable across every book published by Packt
- Copy and paste, print, and bookmark content
- On demand and accessible via a web browser

Table of Contents

Preface

SQLite is still a widely used database for mobile applications on smartphones and tablets. For those with SQL experience, it will be easier to understand and learn what it has to offer and the applications it can be used for. SQLite was released in 2000 has grown to be a well-used database for mobile device development.

Mr. D. Richard Hipp developed it on a battleship while he was at a company called General Dynamics. Initially used as storage, it was then developed using a B-tree implementation, which enhanced it and enabled the storage of rows and transactions.

This book gives you the opportunity to learn elements of SQLite, the mobile database; its interaction with the MAC operating system, Xcode; and the developer IDE for Apple apps and PhoneGap, which enables HTML5. It outlines how easy it is to work with SQLite.

What this book covers

Chapter 1, Introduction to SQL and SQLite, introduces you to the background of Structured Query Language (SQL) and the mobile database SQLite.

Chapter 2, Database Design Concepts, talks about the database concepts in SQLite.

Chapter 3, Administering the Database, introduces you to administering the SQLite database and makes you aware of the different components of this relational database.

Chapter 4, Essentials of SQL, this chapter talks about the essentials of SQL. It will outline the major possibilities with SQL and how it can be used properly on SQLite. This is essential so that you understand how SQL can be used and its limitations and advantages.

Chapter 5, Exposing the C API, deals with the C API and how you can extend its application use and produce the applications that you require using code.

Chapter 6, Using Swift with iOS and SQLite, looks at using the new programming language from Apple, Swift, with SQLite.

Chapter 7, iOS Development with PhoneGap and HTML5, looks at how to use Xcode with PhoneGap to integrate and compile with source code, including HTML5.

Chapter 8, More Features and Advances in SQLite, deals with how SQLite has changed in recent years, how it has advanced to be integrated into a variety of existing technologies, and how its simple easy-to-use formula has guaranteed its popularity with others.

What you need for this book

In this book, the software required will be the following:

- Mac Operating System:
    - OS X 10.9 or later

- Software:
    - Xcode IDE software development environment (version 7.0-7.1.1+) with Swift support
    - Latest version of PhoneGap from `PhoneGap.com`
    - Latest version of Node.js from `https://nodejs.org/en/`

Who this book is for

This book is intended for those who want to learn about the most powerful and flexible mobile database for developing apps in Swift or Objective-C the right way. If you are an expert Objective-C programmer or new to this platform, you'll learn quickly, grasping the code of real-world apps to use Swift effectively.

Conventions

In this book, you will find a number of text styles that distinguish between different kinds of information. Here are some examples of these styles and an explanation of their meaning.

Code words in text, database table names, folder names, filenames, file extensions, pathnames, dummy URLs, user input, and Twitter handles are shown as follows: "This language has a variety of statements but most would recognize the INSERT, SELECT, UPDATE and DELETE statements."

A block of code is set as follows:

```
SELECT parameter1, STTDEV(parameter2)
FROM Table1 Group by parameter1
HAVING parameter1 > MAX(parameter3)
```

Any command-line input or output is written as follows:

```
$ sqlite3 testdatabase.db
```

New terms and **important words** are shown in bold. Words that you see on the screen, for example, in menus or dialog boxes, appear in the text like this: " Then at the bottom of the page, within the **Linked Frameworks and Libraries**, click on the **+** and a modal window will appear."

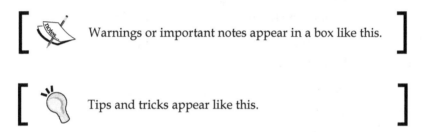

> Warnings or important notes appear in a box like this.

> Tips and tricks appear like this.

Reader feedback

Feedback from our readers is always welcome. Let us know what you think about this book—what you liked or disliked. Reader feedback is important for us as it helps us develop titles that you will really get the most out of.

To send us general feedback, simply e-mail feedback@packtpub.com, and mention the book's title in the subject of your message.

If there is a topic that you have expertise in and you are interested in either writing or contributing to a book, see our author guide at www.packtpub.com/authors.

Customer support

Now that you are the proud owner of a Packt book, we have a number of things to help you to get the most from your purchase.

Downloading the example code

You can download the example code files for this book from your account at
`http://www.packtpub.com`. If you purchased this book elsewhere, you can
visit `http://www.packtpub.com/support` and register to have the files e-mailed
directly to you.

You can download the code files by following these steps:

1. Log in or register to our website using your e-mail address and password.
2. Hover the mouse pointer on the **SUPPORT** tab at the top.
3. Click on **Code Downloads & Errata**.
4. Enter the name of the book in the **Search** box.
5. Select the book for which you're looking to download the code files.
6. Choose from the drop-down menu where you purchased this book from.
7. Click on **Code Download**.

Once the file is downloaded, please make sure that you unzip or extract the folder
using the latest version of:

- WinRAR / 7-Zip for Windows
- Zipeg / iZip / UnRarX for Mac
- 7-Zip / PeaZip for Linux

Downloading the color images of this book

We also provide you with a PDF file that has color images of the screenshots/
diagrams used in this book. The color images will help you better understand the
changes in the output. You can download this file from `http://www.packtpub.com/
sites/default/files/downloads/ Learning_SQLite_for_iOS_ColoredImages.
pdf.pdf`.

Errata

Although we have taken every care to ensure the accuracy of our content, mistakes do happen. If you find a mistake in one of our books—maybe a mistake in the text or the code—we would be grateful if you could report this to us. By doing so, you can save other readers from frustration and help us improve subsequent versions of this book. If you find any errata, please report them by visiting http://www.packtpub.com/submit-errata, selecting your book, clicking on the **Errata Submission Form** link, and entering the details of your errata. Once your errata are verified, your submission will be accepted and the errata will be uploaded to our website or added to any list of existing errata under the Errata section of that title.

To view the previously submitted errata, go to https://www.packtpub.com/books/content/support and enter the name of the book in the search field. The required information will appear under the **Errata** section.

Piracy

Piracy of copyrighted material on the Internet is an ongoing problem across all media. At Packt, we take the protection of our copyright and licenses very seriously. If you come across any illegal copies of our works in any form on the Internet, please provide us with the location address or website name immediately so that we can pursue a remedy.

Please contact us at copyright@packtpub.com with a link to the suspected pirated material.

We appreciate your help in protecting our authors and our ability to bring you valuable content.

Questions

If you have a problem with any aspect of this book, you can contact us at questions@packtpub.com, and we will do our best to address the problem.

1
Introduction to SQL and SQLite

In this chapter, I will introduce you the **Structured Query Language** (SQL) and the mobile database **SQLite**. Whether you are an experienced technologist at SQL or a novice, using this book will help you understand this cool subject, which is gaining momentum. SQLite is a database that is used on a mobile smartphone or tablet, which is local to the device. SQLite has been modified by different vendors to harden and secure it for a variety of uses and applications.

SQLite was released in 2000 and has now grown to be de facto database on a mobile or smartphone. It is an open source piece of software with a low footprint and overheads, which is packed with a **RDBMS (relational database management system)**.

Mr. D. Richard Hipp is the inventor and author of SQLite, which was designed and developed on a battleship while he was with a company called General Dynamics in the US Navy. The programming was built for the **HP-UX** operating system with **Informix** as the database engine. It took many hours in the data to upgrade or install the database software, and was an over-the-top database for this experienced **DBA** (**database administrator**). Mr. Hipp wanted a portable, self-contained, easy-to-use database, which could be mobile, quick to install, and not dependent on the operating system.

Initially, SQLite 1.0 used **gdbm** as its storage system, but later, it was replaced with its own **B-tree** implementation and technology for the database. The B-tree implementation was enhanced to support transactions and store rows of the data with key order. From 2001 onwards, open source family extensions for other languages, such as Java, Python, and Perl, were written to support their applications. The database and its popularity within the open source community and others started growing.

As described in Wikipedia, SQL was as follows:

> *Originally based upon relational algebra and tuple relational calculus, SQL consists of a data definition and manipulation language. The scope of SQL includes data insert, query, update and delete, schema creation and modification, and data access control. Although SQL is often described as, and to a great extent is, a declarative language (4GL), it also includes procedural elements.*

Internationalization supported UTF-16 and UTF-8 and included text-collating sequences in versions 2 and 3 in 2004. It was funded by **AOL (America Online)** in 2004. It works with a variety of browsers that sometimes have in-built support for this technology. For example, there are many extensions that use Chrome or Firefox that allow you to manage the database.

There have been many features added to this product. The future with the growth in mobile phones sets this quick and easy relational database system to quantum leap, where this database's use within the mobile and tablet application space will increase.

SQLite is based on PostgreSQL as a point of reference. SQLite does not enforce any type checking. The schema does not constrain it since the type of value is dynamic, and a trigger will be activated by converting the datatype.

About SQL

In June 1970, a research paper was published by *Dr. E.F. Codd* called *A Relational Model of Data for Large Shared Data Banks*. The **Association of Computer Machinery (ACM)** accepted Codd's data and technology model, which has become the standard of the RDBMS today. IBM Corporation had invented the language called **Structured English Query Language (SEQUEL)**, where the word "English" was dropped to become **SQL**.

SQL has become the standard for the RDMS, which is used by databases such as Oracle, Sybase, and Microsoft's SQL Server.

Today, there are **American National Standards Institute (ANSI)** standards for SQL, and there are many variations of this technology. Among the mentioned manufacturers, there are also others available in the open source world, for example, an SQL query engine, such as **Presto**.

Presto is the distribution engine for SQL under open source, which is made to execute interactive analytic queries. Presto queries are run under databases from a variety of data source sizes—gigabytes to petabytes.

Companies such as Facebook and Dropbox use the Presto SQL engine for their queries and analytics in data warehouse and related applications.

SQL is made up of data manipulation and definition language built with tuple and algebra calculation in a relational format. This language has a variety of statements but most would recognize the INSERT, SELECT, UPDATE, and DELETE statements. These statements form a part of the database schema management process and aid the data and security accesses. SQL includes procedural elements as a part of its setup.

Where does SQLite stand in today's industry?

Companies may use applications, but they are not aware of the SQL engines that drive their data storage and information. Although it had become a standard with the ANSI in 1986, SQL features and functionalities are not 100% portable among different SQL systems. They also require code changes to be useful. These standards are always up for revision to ensure that ANSI is maintained.

There are many industrial and commercial databases, such as Oracle, SQL Server, or DB2, but none of them are as flexible, light, or open source as SQLite. Although smartphones are getting more powerful, you cannot compare them to the processing power of a modern desktop or laptop. SQLite, as its names suggests, is an SQL in a light environment, which is also flexible and versatile. So, at present, the best, light, fully functional, and customized database for mobile, is SQLite.

SQLite cannot be compared to enterprise database engines, such as SQL Server, Oracle, and MySQL. These enterprise database systems provide a centralized and controlled position, whereas SQLite provides local storage on a mobile device. SQLite is effectively based on the economy of size and reliability. It is simple to use, small, robust, and does not compete with these enterprise databases.

SQLite works well with "Internet of Things" as well, because of the no-need-for-human input or administration feature. So, for applications that deal with drones, medical equipment, robots, and sensors, SQL makes an ideal candidate for usage on a variety of mobile applications.

iOS with SQLite

Out of the hundreds of thousands of apps in all the app stores, it would be difficult to find the one that does not require a database of some sort to store or handle data in a particular way. There are different formats of data and datafeeds, but they all require some sort of temporary or permanent storage. A small amount of data may not be applicable, but a medium or large amount of data will require a storage mechanism, such as a database to assist the app.

Using a database such as SQLite with iOS will enable developers to use their existing skills to run their DBMS. For SQLite, there is a C-library that is embedded and available to use with iOS with the **Xcode** IDE.

Apple fully supports SQLite, which uses an include statement as a part of the library call, but developers can also use **FMDB**, which is a **cocoa/objective-C** wrapper around SQLite.

A few advantages of SQLite are that it is fast, lightweight, reliable, uses existing SQL knowledge, is supported by Apple on Mac OS and iOS and by many developers, as well as being integrated without much outside involvement.

The SQLite 3 library is under the general tab once the main project name is highlighted on the left-hand side of the page. Then, at the bottom of the page, within **Linked Frameworks and Libraries**, click on the **+** for a modal window to appear. Enter the word sqlite and select the **libsqlite3.dylib** library, as shown in the following screenshot:

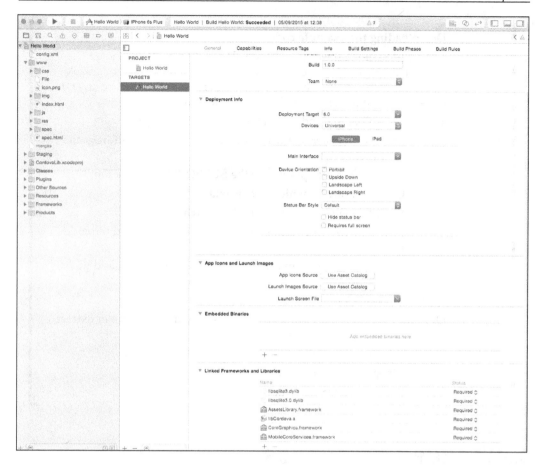

In effect, it is the C++ wrapper, called the `libsqlite3.dylib` library, within the framework section that allows the API to work with SQLite commands.

Before any SQL processes can take place, the database should be opened and ready for querying, and, upon the success of data retrieval, the constant called `SQLITE_OK` should be set to `0`.

Once the C++ wrapper is used and the access to SQLite commands is available, it is an easier process to use SQLite with iOS.

Downloading the example code

You can download the example code files for this book from your account at http://www.packtpub.com. If you purchased this book elsewhere, you can visit http://www.packtpub.com/support and register to have the files e-mailed directly to you.

You can download the code files by following these steps:

- Log in or register to our website using your e-mail address and password.
- Hover the mouse pointer on the **SUPPORT** tab at the top.
- Click on **Code Downloads & Errata**.
- Enter the name of the book in the **Search** box.
- Select the book for which you're looking to download the code files.
- Choose from the drop-down menu where you purchased this book from.
- Click on **Code Download**.

Once the file is downloaded, please make sure that you unzip or extract the folder using the latest version of:

- WinRAR / 7-Zip for Windows
- Zipeg / iZip / UnRarX for Mac
- 7-Zip / PeaZip for Linux

Embedded databases

SQLite has been designed and developed to work and coexist with other applications and processes in its area. RDBMS is tightly integrated with the native application software that requires storing information but is masked, which is hidden from users, and it requires minimal administration or maintenance.

SQLite can work with different APIs hidden from users, and it requires minimal administration or maintenance areas.

The RDMS SQLite will also work with other applications:

- It requires minimal supervision
- There is no network traffic and access is faster since it is a file-based system

- There are no network access conflicts or configurations
- There are no access limitations with privileges or permissions
- There is much reduced overheads

These make it easier and quicker to deploy your applications to app stores or other locations.

Figure 1, seen in this section, shows how different components work seamlessly together in a harmonized way to link up data with the SQLite library and other processes. These show how the Apache and C/C++ processes work together with the SQLite-C library to interface and link with it, so it becomes seamless and integrates with the operating system.

SQLite has been developed and integrated in such a way that it will interface and gel with a variety of applications and multiple solutions. As a lightweight RDBMS, it can stand on its own due to its versatility and is not cumbersome or too complex to benefit your application. It can be used on many platforms, and comes with a binary compatible format, which is easier to dovetail within your mobile application.

The different types of IT professionals will be involved with SQLite, since it holds the data, affects performance, and involves database design, user or mobile interface design specialists, analysts, and consultancy types. These professionals can use their existing knowledge of SQL to quickly grasp SQLite. SQLite can act as both data processor for information, or deal with data in the memory, to perform in an excellent manner.

Figure 1 also outlines how the different software pieces of a jigsaw can interface properly using the C API interface for SQLite with some other programming language code. For example, C or C++ code can be programmed to communicate with the SQLITE C API, which will then talk to the operating system and communicate with the database engine. Another language, such as PHP, can communicate using its own language data objects, which will, in turn, communicate with the SQLite C API and the database.

SQLite is a great database to learn, especially for computer scientists who want to use a tool that can open their minds to investigate caching, B-Tree structures and algorithms, database design architecture, and other concepts.

For more information of how SQLite sits within the other applications on a mobile device, see *Figure 1*:

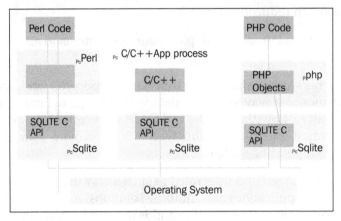

Figure 1: C API interface to SQLite

The architecture of the SQLite database

As a library within the **OS-Interface**, SQLite will have many functions implemented through a program called `tclsqlite.c`. Many technologies and reserved words are used in different languages, but here we have used C language. The core functions are to be found in `main.c`, `legacy.c`, and `vmbeapi.c`. There is also a source code file in C for the TCL language, to avoid any confusion; the prefix of `sqlite3` is used at the beginning of the SQLite library.

The **Tokenizer** code base is found within `tokenize.c`. Its task is to look at the strings that are passed to it and partition or separate them into tokens, which are then passed to the parser. The `tokenize.c` file is included in the code with an include statement and is located in the `sqlite/src/tokenize.c` directory area.

The **Parser** code base is found within `parse.y`. The **Lemon LALR(1)** parser generator is the parser for SQLite; it takes the concept of tokens and assigns them a meaning. To keep within the low-sized footprint of RDBMS, only one C file is used for the parse generator.

The **Code Generator** is then used to create SQL statements from the outputted tokens of the parser. It will produce some virtual machine code that will carry out the work of SQL statements. Several files, such as `attach.c`, `build.c`, `delete.c`, `select.c`, and `update.c`, will handle the SQL statements and syntax.

Virtual machines execute the code that is generated from the Code Generator. It has in-built storage, where each instruction may have up to three additional operands as a part of each code. The source file is called vdbe.c, which is a part of the SQLite database library. Built in is also a computing engine that has been specially created to integrate with the database system.

There are two header files for virtual machines. The **header files** that interface a link between the SQLite libraries are vdbe.h and vdbeaux.c, which have utilities used by other modules. The vdbeapi.c file also connects to virtual machines with sqlite3_bind and other related interfaces. C language routines are called from SQL functions to reference them to the header files. For example, functions such as count() are defined in func.c, and date functions are located in date.c.

B-tree is a type of table implementation used in SQLite, and the C source file is btree.c. The btree.h header file defines the interface of the B-tree system. There is a different B-tree setup for every table and index held within the same file. There is a header portion within btree.c, which will have details of B-tree in a large comment field.

Pager or **Page Cache** using B-tree will ask for data in a fixed size format. The default size is 1024 bytes, but it can be between 512 and 65536 bytes. Commit and Rollback operations, coupled with the caching, reading, and writing of the data, are handled by **Page Cache** or **Pager**. Data locking mechanisms are also handled by **Page Cache**. The C file called page.c is implemented to handle requests within the SQLite library and the header file is pager.h.

The **OS Interface** C file is defined in os.h. It addresses how SQLite can be used on different operating systems, and it becomes transparent and portable to the user, thus becoming a valuable solution for any developer. An abstract layer to handle Win32 and POSIX compliant systems is also kept in place. Different operating systems have their own C file. For example, os_win.c is for Windows, os_unix.c is for Unix; both are coupled with their own os_win.h and os_unix.h header files.

Util.c is the C file that will handle memory allocation and string comparisons. The Utf.c C file will hold Unicode conversion subroutines.

For more information on the architecture of SQLite, see *Figure 2*:

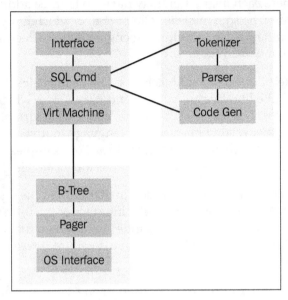

Figure 2: Architecture diagram of SQLite

The Utf.c C file will hold the Unicode data, sort it within the SQL engine, and use the engine as a mechanism for computing data. Since the memory of the device is limited and the database size has the same constraints, the developer has to think outside the box to use these techniques.

These types of memory and resource management formed a part of the approach when the overlay techniques were used in the past and the disk and memory was limited:

```
SELECT parameter1, STTDEV(parameter2)
  FROM Table1 Group by parameter1
  HAVING parameter1 > MAX(parameter3)
```

Features

As part of its standards, SQLite uses and implements most of the SQL-92 standards, but not all the potential features or parts of functionality are used or realized. For example, SQLite uses and implements most of the SQL-92 standards but not all potent columns. The support for triggers is not 100% as it cannot write output to the views.

As mentioned previously, the use of a common datatype for a column is different; most relational database systems assign them to individual values. SQLite will convert a string to an integer if the column's preferred type is an integer. It is a good piece of functionality when bound to this type of scripting language, but the technique is not portable to other RDBMS systems. It also has its criticisms for not having a good data integrity mechanism compared to others, in relation to statically typed columns.

There are some major differences between the two approaches of data: one is **Core Data** and the SQLite way Core Data is similar to having a layer of information between the user interface and the database itself. It does have the advantage of speeding up database interactivity read/write process and saves writing huge queries. While SQLite is a local relational database with its own efficiencies and limitations, it may not suit all applications. Sometimes, due to the speed of a device, Core Data may have the advantage of SQLite directly.

Briefly, your application will have model layer objects, and these are held and managed in a framework, namely, Core Data. It manages the life cycle of an object within iOS. This is just some background information to show how data can be read from databases and the speed at which this takes place.

The advantages of using SQLite

A few advantages of using SQLite are listed here:

- SQLite does have a data constraints feature and can edit or drop tables without loading them into memory.
- SQLite works on the data stored on the disk and is slower compared to Core Data.
- Core Data, on the other hand, does not have data constraints, and can be implemented using the app's business logic instead.
- In order to update or drop a table, the entire table has to be loaded up.
- Core Data is quick to create records/rows but slower to save the data.
- Core Data does have another advantage where it operates and works in the memory, and the data has to be loaded from the disk to memory.
- Core Data works with objects based in the memory, or can be accessed using the standard slower disk method.
- Core Data will work on non-transactional, single user, or single-threaded methods. SQLite's function is to fetch and store data using its file database system. It operates by storing the data on the disk where the data is incrementally or minimally loaded.

- Effectively, the data can be transactional, multiuse, and thread-safe. It saves data to the disk and is mostly resilient to crashes. It is slower if you have to create hundreds of thousands of rows, but it does have data constraints, such as unique keys.

- SQLite has bindings to many languages such as Basic, C, C#, C++, Java, JavaScript, Lua, PHP, Objective-C, Python, Ruby, and TCL. Its popularity with the open source community and usage by customers and developers has enabled its growth to continue.

- This lightweight RDMS can be used on Google Chrome, Firefox, Safari, Opera, and Android browsers and has middleware support using ADO. NET, ODBC, COM (ActiveX), and XULRunner. It also has a support for web application frameworks, such as Django (Python based), Ruby on Rails, and Bugzilla (Mozilla). There are other applications, such as Adobe Photoshop Light and Skype that use SQLite. It is also a part of Windows 8, Symbian OS, Android, and OpenBSD operating systems.

- Apart from not having the large overheads of other database engines, SQLite has a major enhancement, known as the EXPLAIN keyword, with its manifest typing.

- For controlling constraint conflicts, the REPLACE and ON CONFLICT statements are used.

- Within the same query, multiple independent databases can be accessed using the DETACH and ATTACH statements.

- New SQL functions and collating sequences can be created using the predefined APIs, which offer much more flexibility.

- As there is no configuration required, SQLite just does the job and works.

- No lists, such as the REPLACE and ON CONFLICT procedures, are required.

- There is no need to initialize, stop, restart, or start server processes, and no administrator is required to create the database with proper access controls or security permits.

- After any failure, no user actions are required to recover the database, since it is self-repairing.

- SQLite is more advanced than previously thought. Unlike other RDMS, it does not require a server setup via a server to serve up data or incur network traffic costs. There is no TCP/IP calls, nor frequent communication backward or forward.

- SQLite is direct; the operating system process deals with database access to its file and controls database writes and reads with no middle-man process handshaking.

- By having no server backend, the process of installation, configuration, or administration is reduced significantly, and access to the database is granted to programs that require this type of data operation. This is an advantage in one way, but it is also a disadvantage for security and protection from data-driven misuse, data concurrency, or data row locking mechanisms.

- It also allows the database to be accessed several times by different applications at the same time.

- It supports a form of portability for the cross platform database file that can be located with the database file structure. The database file can be updated on one system and copied to another on either 32 bit or 64 bit with different architectures; this does not make a difference to SQLite.

- The usage of different architectures and the promises of developers to keep the file system stable and compatible with previous, current, and future developments will allow this database to grow and thrive. SQLite databases do not need to upload old data to new, formatted, and upgraded databases; it just works.

- By having a single disk file for the database, the information can be copied on a USB and shared or just reused on another device very quickly by keeping all the information intact.

- Another feature of this portable database, SQLite, is its size, which can start on a single 512-byte page and expand to 2,147,483,646 pages at 65,536 bytes per page, or in bytes 140,737,488,224,256, which equates to about 140 terabytes. Most other RDBMS are much larger, but IBM's Cloudscape is small, with a 2 MB jar file, but still larger than SQLite.

- The Firebird alternative's client (frontend) library is about 350 KB, whereas the Berkeley Oracle database is around 450 KB, without the SQL support, and with one simple key/value pair's option.

- This advanced portable database system and its source code is in the public domain. However, there are open source license issues and controls for some test code and documentation.

- This is great news for developers who might want to code up new extensions or database functionality that works with their programs, which could be made into a "product extension" for SQLite.

- You cannot have this sort of access to SQL source code around since everything has a patent, limited access, or just no access.

- There are signed affidavits by developers to disown any copyright interest in the SQLite code. SQLite is different because it is just not governed or ruled by copyright law, which monitors the way a software should really work or be used.

Using the small allocation with variable length records, applications run faster, database access is quicker, manifest typing is used, and the database is small and nimble.

The ease of using this RDBMS makes it easier for most programmers at an intermediate level to create applications using this technology, with its detailed documentation and examples.

Other RDBMS are internally complex, with links to data structures and objects. SQLite comprises a virtual machine language that uses the EXPLAIN reserved word in front of a query.

The virtual machine has increased and benefitted this database engine by providing an excellent process or controlled environment between the backend (where the results are computed and outputted), and frontend (where the SQL is parsed and executed).

The SQL implementation language is comparable to other RDBMS, especially with its lightweight base, and it supports recursive triggers and requires the FOR/EACH ROW behavior. The FOR EACH statement is not currently supported, but functionality cannot be ruled out in the future.

As described so far in this chapter, SQLite is a nimble and easy-to-use database that developers can engage with quickly, use existing skills, and output systems to mobile devices and tablets far easier than ever before. With the help of HTML5 and other JavaScript frameworks, the advancement of SQL and number of SQLite installations will take a quantum leap.

Working with SQLite

The website for SQLite is available at www.sqlite.org, where you can download all the binaries for the database, documentation, and source code, which works on operating systems such as Linux, Windows, and MAC OS X.

The SQLite **share library** or **DLL** is the library to be used for the Windows operating system and can be installed or seen via Visual Studio with the C++ language. So, the developer can write the code using the library that is presently linked in reference via the application. When the execution has taken place, the DLL will load and all the references in the code will link to those in the DLL at the right time.

The SQLite3 **command-line program — CLP —** is a self-contained program that has all the components to run at the command line.

It also comes with an extension for TCL. So within TCL, you can connect and update the SQLite database. SQLite downloads come with the TAR version for Unix systems, and the ZIP version for Windows systems.

The examples of using SQLite with iOS

The following is a simple application on how to use iOS with the SQLite database with Xcode. It outlines the basic steps of creating an application and database, and selecting data.

To get started, let's start Xcode and create a template using the **Single View Application** choice, as shown in the following screenshot:

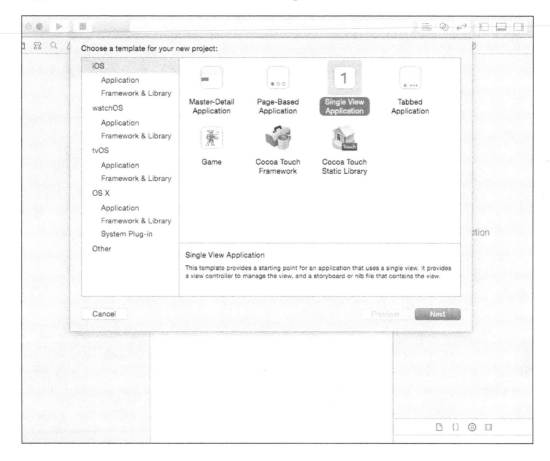

Click on the **Next** button to proceed to the next screen in this process. In the product name field, enter `SimpleCalculator` for the language, and select **Swift**. For the devices field, select **iPhone**. Then, click on the **Next** button to move onto the next screen, as shown in the following screenshot:

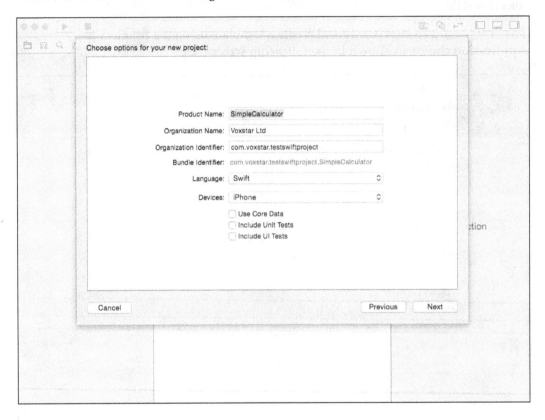

In the following screenshot, select the directory where the code will reside. Now, we can view what the Xcode developer tool has created. Then, select a device to display the information; in our case, use the iPhone 6s.

See the directory for the source code, as shown in the following screenshot:

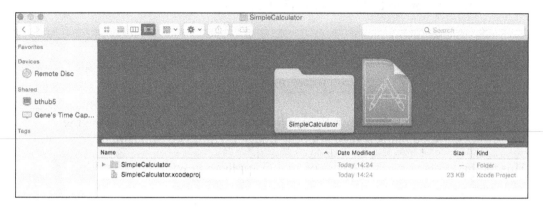

The following is a screenshot showing the SimpleCalculator application opened in Xcode. Select the **iPhone 6s** option as the device to develop on:

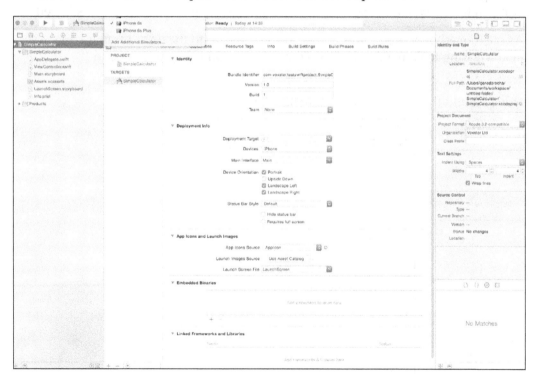

Next, click on the **Play** button that will compile and build the application as shown here in both images, and a blank screen will appear:

The preceding screenshot shows the application to be built, and the following screenshot shows a blank screen after the image is compiled and run.

This method gets you to the basics of an iOS application with Swift working as a canvas.

In this brief example, we will use `SQLiteDB.swift` and `String-Extras.swift` to work with the SQLite database, including the `Bridging-Header.h` file. In the **Build Settings** option, view **Objective-C Bridging Header** and double-click on it, and bridge it to `Bridging-Header.h`, and you can also drag it to show that it is linked.

As mentioned previously, add `libsqlite3.0.dylib` to the linked frameworks by navigating to **General | Linked Frameworks and Libraries**; then, add `Libsqlite3.0.dylib`.

Now, rebuild the project to show that it's working:

Click on the **Simulator** button, and then click on **Quit** to stop the current compiled simulator program. The program will compile with no problems. Next, a database instance has to be created as shown in the following code. The `SQLite.DB.query` method is used to execute these commands:

- First an instance is required:

```
let testdb = SQLiteDB.sharedInstance()
```

- To run this query, the following code is used with the `SQLiteDB.query` way:

```
var theresult = testdb.query("select * from people where county =
'Berks'", parameters: nil)
for row in result
{
    println(row["name"]!.asString())
}
```

- To delete a record for example, follow the following piece of code:

```
testdb.execute("delete from people where county =
'Bucks' ", parameters: nil)
```

Summary

In this chapter, you read the history of SQL, the impact of relational databases, and the use of a mobile SQL database, namely, SQLite. This chapter outlined the history and beginnings of SQLite and how it has grown to be the most used database on mobile devices so far. In the next chapter, you will learn about the components of database concepts and how to design an SQLite database. The next chapter will show you the basic elements of design for an SQLite database.

2
Database Design Concepts

In this chapter, you will learn about SQLite's database concepts. Just as with most databases, SQLite too can add data using the SQL command called INSERT. It can also modify data using the UPDATE command and remove data using the DELETE command. It can also retrieve data using the SELECT command.

These four commands form the base line for any SQL database RDMS in the market. This set of commands manipulate the data, and this type of searching is called a **query**.

Database essentials

This persistent and structured way of storing data is simply called a database, and the data itself is stored using tables. Each table consists of columns and rows, with a look and feel similar to **Microsoft Excel**.

SQLite is based on the C language and a related API (RDBMS) in the market. The C language, for example, is easy to understand and is based on the fundamentals of database design with RDBMS. However, learning the actual API will benefit your skills and understanding.

In order to understand the API, you will have to learn the components that make up the database to improve your knowledge. Understanding data structures, SQL transactions, concurrency, and data-locking mechanisms, and creating good optimized queries will help you design great database systems.

Lastly, you need to put this understanding into some software code for the app you write and see how it is integrated and executed. The API language extension will be discussed further in this chapter.

The design objective of SQLite was to keep the role of administration and operation easy to use and simple to manage. SQLite is **ACID** (**atomicity**, **consistency**, **isolation**, and **durability**) compliant, and is fully transactional using **T-SQL**.

As a part of the design, the SQLite database has a variety of datatypes like most databases. One of the types is the INTEGER type that has 64 bit numeric values. This database uses 64 bit numeric values and the data is stored in 1, 2, 3, 4, 5, 6, or 8 bytes. The TEXT type encoding uses UTF-8 for storing it in the database. The BLOB datatype can be stored directly, with a default size of 1,000,000,000 bytes.

SQLite also uses the REAL type, which is a 64 bit floating point value, and there is the standard NULL value as well. The REAL type will be applied to the FLOAT, DOUBLE, and REAL datatypes. The TEXT type applies to the NCHAR, NVARCHAR, TEXT, and VARCHAR datatypes. The NUMERIC type applies to DATE, DATETIME, and BOOLEAN. SQLite also uses **CRUD** (**Create, Read, Update,** and **Delete**), and this database is *not* case sensitive.

The statements are shown as follows:

- The CREATE statement is used to create new tables in the SQLite database. The basic syntax and a simple example of CREATE TABLE is shown here. The CREATE TABLE statement has a database name that is fixed. It is followed by a table name, which has a start and close bracket. Within this statement, there is a list of column(s) to be created, starting with their names and datatypes, as shown in the following:

  ○ ```
    CREATE table database-name. table-name(column1
    datatype, column2 datatype, column3, datatype, PRIMARY
    KEY column1);
    ```

- The INSERT statement will have a table name followed by a set of columns on the first half. The second half will have the variables, where the data coming from that will be inserted into the table. It is important to ensure that the programmer uses the same datatype as the column created; otherwise, there will be an error or a warning:

  ○ ```
    INSERT into table-name(column1,column2,column3) VALUES(v
    ariable1,variable2,variable3);
    ```

- The UPDATE statement is used to update records or rows within a table. The UPDATE statement will have a table name, followed by a set of columns to update on the left-hand side, and some data variables on the right-hand side, as shown in the following:

  ○ ```
    UPDATE table-name SET column1=variable1,
    column2=variable2, column3=variable3) [where variable4 =
    10];
    ```
    ```

- The SELECT statement is used to select information, records, or rows within a table. This is shown in *Figure 7*. The SELECT statement will have a set of columns on the first half, followed by a table name and a condition, as shown here:
  - ° SELECT column1, column2, column3 FROM table-name WHERE column1 > 10;

- The DELETE statement is used to delete records or rows within a table. This is shown here. The DELETE statement will have a set of columns on the first half, followed by a table and any condition:
  - ° DELETE from table-name where column1 >10;

The extension and core APIs are the sections that form the API made with the C language. The core database carries out functions such as processing SQL syntax and connecting to the database. Other tasks, such as error trapping and string formatting, are also dealt with the core API. As mentioned earlier, the extension API allows programmers to add or extend the current API with a new functionality that will add the functionality that does not exist presently or as a current definition with the SQLite program.

Although data structures are outlined, as mentioned previously, using the tokenizer or parser, their importance is reduced, since coders are interested in other parts, such as the connectivity syntax, parameters, or current functions, and not the internals of the products. In order to write some good code, programmers must be clued up on SQLite locks, transactions, and the API itself.

Although not a part of the API itself, the **pager** and **B tree** parts of the SQLite system contribute heavily as a part of locking and transactions mechanisms.

There are eight methods and two objects that make up the C/C++ interface part of the SQLite database system. The two objects are: sqlite3, which is the actual database connection object, and sqlite3_stmt, which is the prepare statement object.

The eight methods comprise the following:

- sqlite3_exec(): This is a wrapper function
- sqlite3_close(): This is a destructor for sqlite3
- sqlite3_finalize():This is a destructor for sqlite3_stmt
- sqlite3_column(): This holds the column values for sqlite3_stmt
- sqlite3_step():This allows you to step to the next result row and is an advancement of sqlite3_stmt

- `sqlite3_bind()`: This is how SQL is broken down into parameters from the stored application data

- `sqlite3_prepare()`:This is a part of the constructor for `sqlite3_stmt`, where byte code is produced from SQL that has been compiled, so it can carry out the SQL statements (`SELECT`, `UPDATE`)

- `sqlite3_open()`: This is the constructor of `sqlite3`, which allows a connection to an existing or a new SQLite database

Initially, SQLite was easy to learn and had only five C/C++ interfaces, but now, it has grown in size, functionality, and interfaces to over 200 APIs. It can be daunting to use 200 APIs, but SQLite has been designed in such a way that you only use the API, but now, it has grown in size and function.

These six core interfaces, once mastered, will give programmers a great understanding of SQLite. They are listed here:

- `SQLite3_open()`: This function makes a connection to the SQLite database and, once successful, a database connection object will be returned. None of the other interfaces will be available until the `SQLite3_open()` interface has been set up. They require a starting point, or a reference to a database, and a database connection object.

- `SQLite3_prepare()`: This function will convert and set up SQL statements into a formatted object, and the output will be a pointer that will be stored in reference to that object. In order to progress, this interface requires a database connection object produced by the `SQLite3_open()` function.

- `SQLite3_column()`: This interface does not interrogate the SQL, it just produces a prepared statement. This interface is now not the preferred choice for new applications, but the alternative `SQLite3_prepare_V2()` interface must be used.

- `SQLite3_step()`: This interface will look at the prepared statement as set up by the `SQLite3_prepare()` function and will return a single column from the current record set. This is not purely a function, but a placeholder for the type of functions that return values with different datatypes. These form a part of the results set. There are other functions that are a part of the `sqlite3_column()` setup, and they are, `sqlite3_column_blob()`, `sqlite3_column_bytes()`, `sqlite3_column_bytes16()`, `sqlite3_column_count()`, `sqlite3_column_double()`, `sqlite3_column_int()`, `sqlite3_column_int64()`, `sqlite3_column_text()`, `sqlite3_column_type()`, and `sqlite3_column_value()`.

- `SQLite3_finalize()`: This function is the interface that destroys the prepared statement to stop any memory leaks in the system.

- `SQLite3_close()`: This interface will shut any database connection and prepared statements before closing or ceasing operations.

There are other routines, such as `sqlite3_bind()` and `sqlite3_reset()`, that enable prior statements to be used again and again. Usually, statements are created, prepared, and destroyed once, but the aforementioned routines can be used at multiple instances.

SQLite has the `sqlite3_config()` interface that is first selected before any connections to the database are initiated. This interface will have the ability to set global changes for the database. It can also allocate memory, set up allocators for real-time embedded systems, and page caching for a predefined application usage. It can also make adjustments for different treading models.

This database system is flexible, and using `sqlite3_create_collation()`, `sqlite3_create_function()`, `sqlite3_create_module()`, and `sqlite3_vfs_register()` functions will allow the SQLite system to have a new proprietary functionality on the RDBMS. For example, the `sql_create_function()` function will create additional functionality for aggregate or scalar purposes. These are `sqlite3_agreegate_context()`, `sqlite3_result()`, `sqlite3_user_data()`, and `sqlite3_value()`.

These are the standard built-in functionalities of the SQLite system that prove how flexible the system can be to programmers. It is this flexibility, together with the technology that has helped it grow and cultivate to a place where it has become the best SQL database for mobiles today.

In addition, there are many other interfaces and functions that are too many to include in this book. They can be found under the C/C++ interface specification of this product.

SQLite, by default, will do most of the tasks required by programmers, users, or DBAs. Programmers are always looking to go beyond the normal bounds of the relational database system, or take advantage of these extensions to fulfill their solution requirements.

Reasons for using SQLite

There are many features that make SQLite a great database for mobile technologies. For example, there is no administration or configuration involved, the transactions are atomic, the database is self-contained in a single cross-platform file, and it holds advanced features, such as table expressions and partial indexes. The reasons for using SQLite are listed here:

It has a small, versatile, and easy-to-use API. It is very standard-compliant and is written using the ANSI-C compliant. There are no external dependencies on any external programs or services, and the code is well commented. The source code is in the public domain and has a standalone **CLI (command-line interface)** at its disposal. It is cross-platform compliant, works with Mac, Linux, BSD, Android, Solaris, VxWorks, and Windows (WinCE, Win32, WinRT).

Its code footprint is very small, less than 500 kB when configured. The amount of application range that uses this database is huge. Almost all the products can have or have the need for a database that SQLite can handle.

It may not have all the bells and whistles of an enterprise system, but it is very flexible and easily available. SQLite is used by a variety of companies such as Adobe, Dropbox, Skype, and many more users.

SQLite is tested independently with its own test facilities and criteria. There are tests for memory usage, crash and power loss, fuzz tests boundary value and disable optimization tests, regression tests, and behavior checks among others. The test harnesses are also independently developed and verified.

The testing process for SQLite is well tested and matured, and the TCL tests are built using the TCL Scripting language. The test harnesses are made using the C code that creates the TCL interface. There are over 800 files of test scripts that hold over 10 gigabytes of data and over 30,000 test cases.

There are also SQL logic tests that run SQL statements against other database engines, such as SQL Server, PostgreSQL, Oracle, and SQLite itself. These form a part of the SLT (SQL Logic Test) that runs over 7 million queries and 1 gigabyte of test data as a part of the testing load.

Also, there are many types of stress and performance testing, including anomaly tests, which include the behavior of SQLite on a variety of checks and see how it performs when errors occur. All the tests are run on all the platforms that SQLite works with. There is a subset of testing scripts that are used as a quick test; however, over 200,000 test cases—enough to capture any errors, or misfit code—can still be executed quickly.

There are also tests for checking the memory usage that look at memory allocation and the use of the `malloc()` function. All the SQL databases use the `malloc()` function to allocate and release memory. Since SQLite is heavily used in embedded systems, it is required to handle errors in a graceful manner.

I/O testing is carried out to ensure that I/O errors are handled and dealt with properly. These issues maybe with regard to network errors, configuration, disk issues, or permissions. Errors are created to see their effects and to see how the software handles them.

A **virtual file system (VFS)** is also used to simulate the database crashing as part of the testing procedures. There are also simulations using power failures, so any measurement can be recorded. The crash test processes are completed separately.

There are also fuzz tests that take care to see that SQLite works with odd and different inputs and all the results are checked. Processes are spawned and the VFS is used to simulate crashes. In addition to the standard fuzz test, there are fuzz tests for SQL that look at the syntax and inputting to the database to check the responses and results. These form a part of the TCL testing, and there are over 100,000 fuzz tests. All the results are recorded and analyzed.

All branch tests for this database are 100% tested and measured. There are also measurements and tests to ensure that any automatic resource leaks are detected, noted, and dealt with. Usually, resource leaks occur when, in certain circumstances, resources are allocated by the malloc() function; but they are not released when other processes may require the same resource or some form of shared resource. When the resource is not freed or released as instructed, then it leads to resource leakage.

SQLite also has dynamic analysis that checks the internal and external SQLite code while the code is being executed or is in use online. This type of analysis is used to ensure that SQLite has the best availability and quality for users.

Valgrind is the simulator of the Linux binary and x86 environments. As a simulator, it is much slower, but it is effective. **Memsys2** has a memory allocation system that is pluggable; it uses the malloc() and free() functions. If SQLite is compiled with the SQLite_MEMDEBUG compile-time option, then, as a part of the debugging memory allocator, a larger wrapper is used around the malloc(), realloc(), and free() functions. If Memsys2 is used, it looks for memory allocation errors at runtime.

There are the mutex subsystems in SQLite that use the sqlite3_mutex_held() and sqlite3_mutex_notheld() function. This is a pluggable subsystem, and these two interfaces detect whether a mutex subsystem has a particular thread. SQLite uses the assert() set of functions to ensure that multithreaded applications work correctly within the database system.

SQLite uses a rollback journal to ensure that all the changes on the database are recorded before actually making changes to the database. SQLite has to work with different conditions so that it does not conflict or cause undetermined or odd behavior that must be managed. Since the code is developed in C, it may work with many implementations and libraries during development, but in the production area, it must confirm and may not work sometimes.

So, checks such as a shifting using a negative number may be tried, or trying the `memcpy()` function to copy buffers that are overlapping and checking that unsigned or signed variables apply to `char` datatypes. To cope with, and cater for these issues, the compiler (**GCC**) may use the `-fraction` to within the test suites.

Before the code is released, it goes through a ping and checks that unsigned or signed, or analyzed and compile time errors will be checked before going forward. Both the connections — **Connection 1** and **Connection 2** — are shown as follows:

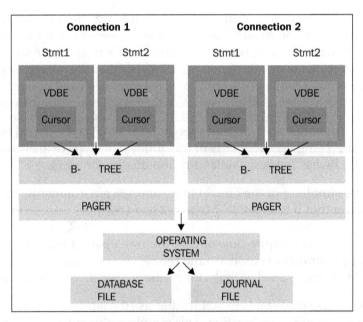

Figure 9: SQLite object model with C API

Figure 9 outlines the views that a programmer will look at — B-tree and pager, rather than components such as tokenizers or parser. *Figure 9* outlines the relationship between the components. To know SQLite properly, programmers must understand the locks, API, and transactions of SQLite.

As *Figure 9* illustrates, pager and B-tree access is forbidden, but important within locks and transactions. The connection to the database and SQL statements is most important when the API has many data structures. For example, a connection to any SQLite database is held as one transaction and also as one connection to the RDMS. A SQL statement is internally represented in the form of a **virtual database of engine** (**VDBE**) byte code.

With the B-tree and pager components of SQLite, it will support many database objects within each connection, as shown in *Figure 9*. Every database object has a B-tree object, which has a relationship with a pager object. The SQL code (SQL statements) within each connection are shown in *Figure 9*. Every database object has a B-tree object, which has a relationship.

When B-tree requires information, it prompts the pager component to get the data from the database. The pager component will move the data into its memory buffer, and the B-tree component will then associate it via its cursor to retrieve and view the data.

Executing SQL statements and commands is a part of the main piece of the API that has two methods, which are either prepared or wrapped queries. If the page is modified by the cursor, the original page/data must be kept just in case of a database rollback. The pager is very important and has to deal with write and read events to and from the RDBMS.

A transaction is set up once an operation is in place. For example, a database connection setup will effectively be considered as one transaction. Also remember that a connection cannot have more than one transaction open or available at any given time.

Therefore, SQL statements from a standard connection will work on the same transaction. If the conditions of your program require more than one statement in different transactions, you have to engage in using multiple connections, as illustrated in *Figure 9*.

It is very important to know how to set up a database connection from the application to the SQLite database. If there is no connection, then any of the commands used to retrieve, update, or insert data are useless. The connection statement will define the data process and its name and will set up a transaction to allow the data to pass to the database and back. Once a connection is made, the rest of the process sets up the database interactivity. It is not a difficult task to complete, but setting up a database is important to learn, because it is the starting point of all database activities and applications.

Database connections

The `sqlite3_open()` C API function is used to open a connection to the database and is held in a single operating system file. This function actually opens the file, and thus, a secure connection is made that is not shared. If the memory option is used, then the database will be created in **random access memory (RAM)**, once the connection is established. The database will then be removed and deleted from RAM when the connection closed.

SQLite will attempt to open an existing database, and if an entered database name does not exist, then it will assume that the programmer wants to create one. SQLite is clever if you want to create a database and then close it without any operation, such as creating a table: it will not actually spend resources creating the database, only an empty file will exist:

```
sqlite3 aFile.db "create table aTable(field1 int); drop table aTable;"
```

The preceding statement will create the required default file with a table and will then drop/delete it, leaving a clean database without any tables. This is possibly the neatest way to show an empty database.

When opening the SQLite database, the programmer or database administrator can specify the size of the page in different ranges from 512 to 32,768 bytes. By default, SQLite will use a 1,024 byte page size. For a better performance, the developer may consider a page size of his SQLite database equal to the operating system's page size, which will make operations much more efficient.

It all depends on the type of application you are going to design; paying attention to the detail on the type of columns, sizes, and types, which will gear a table and database design to be more efficient and perform well. If the application you are dealing with has large binary data for example, the database page size will increase to match the loading or selecting of data. The `page_size` parameter is used as a part of the database page sizing for each database.

Preparing queries

These are the eight methods and two objects that form the SQLite interface. These are the basic list of functions that each user/reader must be aware of when using SQLite in code. These statements don't change, nor does their functionality. These are the key statements to ensure that users are aware of the name, format, and where these functions are used:

- `sqlite3`: Database connection object, made by `sqlite3_open()`, killed by `sqlite3_close()`

- `sqlite3_stmt`: Preparation statement object, made by `sqlite3_prepare()`, killed by `sqlite3_finalize()`

- `sqlite3_open()`: Opens the database (new or existing) and uses constructor `sqlite3`

- `sqlite3_prepare()`: Compiles some SQL text into byte code to perform updating or querying tasks and is the constructor of `sqlite3_stmt`

- `sqlite3_bind()`: Application data is stored into the parameters of the original SQL

- `sqlite3_step()`: The further advancement of `sqlite3_stmt` onto the next row or completion

- `sqlite3_column()`: The current row result outlining column values for `sqlite3_stmt`

- `sqlite3_finalize()`: `sqlite3_stmt` destructor

- `sqlite3_close()`: `sqlite3` destructor

- `sqlite3_exec()`: A wrapper function that works for one or many SQL statements using `sqlite3_prepare()`, `sqlite3_step()`, `sqlite3_finalize()`, and `sqlite3_column()`

The `sqlite3_prepare_v2()` function is the one used to prepare and execute SQL statements. The prepare function is the method that SQLite uses as a part of the following three-stage process:

1. First is the preparation stage, next the execution stage, and then the finalization stage. On the preparation side (first step), the components, as explained in *Chapter 1, Introduction to SQL and SQLite*, outline the parser, tokenizer, and code maker to investigate the SQL and make a statement using the `sqlite3_prepare_v2()` function working with the compiler. Then, a handle is created with byte code from the `sqlite3_stmt` function that collates and uses relevant resources for the statement to execute.

2. Secondly, VDBE within SQLite will take the byte code and execute it using the C API. The `sqlite3_step()` will work with (VDBE) to go through the byte code looking at locking resources as required. Different statements will work differently in VDBE, but for the SELECT statements as an example, using `sqlite3_step()` as part of a result set, SQLITE_ROW() will be set and the process will go through the whole dataset until SQLITE_DONE is reached. Other statements in the set including UPDATE, INSERT, and DELETE will be directly executed within VDBE.

3. The third step is the final one where the resources to VDBE are closed; the `sqlite3_finalize()` function does this. Once the `sqlite3_finalize()` function is executed and resources are free, the program comes to an end via the VDBE and the statement handle is closed as well.

Parameterized SQL

Using SQL within C code and the API will involve parameterized SQL—the way to include data placeholders in an SQL statement. These are the two types of parameterized binding: named and positional. See *Figure 10* for more details on how these types of parameterized binding are used. The first statement is positional where its position is located or marked by a question mark, and these positions are based on the number of columns.

The real variable names setup in the programmable language, such as C or Java, as shown in the second insert statement in *Figure 10*, outlines the named parameters that use a colon as a prefix to indicate it on an SQL statement. By default, NULL is used as a default value if there is no value for it to be bound to.

Once a statement is bound, you can call on it again more than once without wasting the performance or time to recompile it again.

The whole idea of using parameterized SQL is to reuse the same code with different parameters without recompiling. It saves on resources and time, and improves efficiency. This allows the existing code to be reused several times if the design allows it, to save on more code and improve efficiency. If you use quotes or characters for plurals as an example, SQLite, by default, will escape the characters and insert the right data and convert it properly.

It also stops SQL injections, SQL penetrations, and easy syntax issues or errors. The SQL injection to a company is a security vulnerability, which allows a hacker to trick the system into adding or modifying data where access is not granted. On a browser where the address of a website is seen, the data input is sometimes added without any encryption, or no data checking is carried out at the backend or frontend to allow penetration. SQL injections, as illustrated and explained in *Figure 12*, show that an open piece of code that relies on an input using a `%s` string, can be regarded as opened, and can impact the data in the database:

```
insert into details (id, name, address, country, postcode), values (?,?,?,?,?);

insert into property(id, name, description, location, value) (:id, :name,:desc,:location,
:value);
```

Figure 10: Using parameterized SQL

The following snippet shows how a statement can be compiled using one set of parameters; using the `function _reset()` method will allow the same compiled SQL code to be used again with different parameters:

```
#  example of using reset  - START
db1= open('property.db')
sql_statement= db1.prepare('insert into property_info(id,property_
id,desc) values(:id,:pr_id,:desc)')
sql_statement.bind('id','100')
sql_statement.bind('property_id','1')
sql_statement.bind('desc','this is a test')
sql_statement.step()
# Reuse existing compiled parameters
sql_statement.reset()
sql_statement.bind('id','200')
sql_statement.bind('property_id','2')
sql_statement.bind('desc','this is a test again')
# End
statement_sql.finalize()
db1.close()
```

Error handling

Handling errors is mandatory when writing systems, especially if it is for mobile devices; so, attention to detail and catching issues with code is vital. The `SQLITE_BUSY` and `SQLITE_ERROR` functions are used by programmers to notify and trap errors, and store them for a later analysis.

For example, `SQL_ERROR` is activated when resources such as locks cannot be granted or are not available, whereas the `SQL_BUSY` covers issues with transactions and related matters. Another function called `sqlite3_errcode()` will handle any general SQLite error. These methods and functions are the standard way of handling errors with SQLite.

Queries within the db.exec statement

The `sqlite3_get_table()` function is used to execute SQL statements that actually return data, such as the SELECT statement, but the `sqlite3_exec()` function is a one-way traffic execution and does not return any data, for example, the INSERT statement. See the following code for more information:

```
db1= open('property.db')
sql_statement= db1.exec("insert into
property_info(id,property_id,desc) values(1,2,'Property Description
1')")
sql_statement= db1.exec("insert into
property_info(id,property_id,desc) values(2,2,'Property
Description 2')")
```

SQL injection attacks

Another issue with SQLite and SQL statements generally is **SQL injection attacks**. These can deface websites, result in data corruption, and also affect the reputation of your website and its customers. If the input to SQL parameters is direct, then a weakness could be penetrable. SQL data input must be checked and filtered to allow no one to change the current statement with data elements or even replace SQL statements to perform corrupt acts. This can be done using this statement:

```
SELECT * from property where property_name='%s';
```

The preceding code shows that an injection can take place where %s is the input string, and it can be changed to be something else, thus changing the outcome result. To protect SQL, constrain the input, use parameters with stored procedures, and use parameters with dynamic SQL to reduce the threats.

To prevent your website from being used for XSS or XSRF attacks, disallow the HTML tags in text input provided by users by using functions to find and strip tags.

Creating user-defined functions

The benefit of using SQLite over other small databases is its flexibility to engage with the extension API side by creating your own user-defined function. If you are familiar with creating your own function in a language such as Java or C, for example, then extending the natural SQLite database will not be difficult. The following code outlines how this can be done using the C API:

```
void test_function(sqlite3_content* tmp_value, int tmp_assign,
sqlite3_value** values)
```

```
{
/* Respond back Text or reply */
    const char *tmp_string ="Test String - Hello World";

/* Set value to be returned */
sqlite3_result_text(tmp_value,tmp_string,strlen(tmp_string),SQL_
STATIC);
}
Execute it by creating function using - sqlite3_create_
function(db1,"test_function", 0,test_function);
```

Transactions and locks

Transactions and lock states form a part of the makeup of the API and its functions.

Although difficult to control in their entirety, locks and transactions are interlinked with queries within SQLite and most database systems. The key to better transactions involves the programmer writing good SQL code, ensuring that it will perform well, and catering for possible errors and issues during the journey so that the application does not crash or leave the user in the lurch. Another issue with locks will relate to which resources you need. Sometimes, it could be a badly written code that does not use autocommit or is holding an exclusive lock to a table and another part of your process, and you can't update it, as an example. So, it is very important for the programmer to gauge, learn the API, and understand how locking and transaction strategies will work to produce a smooth and good app.

By default, autocommit is used in SQLite where transactions cycles start and end, which are controlled by programmers and statements used for the app. Each SQL command will run in its own transaction since autocommit is used. However, within a transaction, especially using a begin command, the programmer has to manually call a rollback, or a commit to update the database. Sometimes, a locking strategy such as this may cause SQL violations or errors, which has to be handled by the error handling code within the app.

In terms of passwords, as a programmer or designer, do not store password, such as database passwords, in any clear text or script that may be accessed by any user. For example, in a directory to a web server, a source file can be compromised.

Application authentication should be done on two levels with heavy type password formats so that access is not compromised, especially with technology, such as spyware that looks into compromising your system. The data can be encrypted when database authorization provisions do not offer sufficient protection, which is initially required.

Transactions – reading/writing

When a SELECT statement is used within SQLite, it moves from a default status of UNLOCKED to SHARED, and once the statement is committed, it reverts to UNLOCKED. There are several states for transaction lock states and locking works when there is autocommit on or transactional control with autocommit off within a begin/end statement arrangement. When there is some contention, the transactional locking states may alter from UNLOCKED to SHARED, RESERVED, or EXCLUSIVE.

If an update is to take place, the programmer may code it so that an EXCLUSIVE lock is used. This stops updates from other processes, just until the job has been done and the lock is released. In this case, the programmer must also code and put up a message or write to the log file; if this happens, auditors or database administrators will have an audit trail of events during the lifetime of an application. It is a very good practice to do so.

Designing for SQLite

Generally, programmers will think that because database systems are huge or work best in enterprise, it will be the same for SQLite and the mobile environment. Remember when the app is released; ensure that SQLite is built in with some basic data for the user to start. Ensure that the data can be dynamically populated easily. This will form a part of a great data access strategy and format, which should be replicated across all of your applications.

As mentioned previously, security to your data is mandatory, and requirements around privacy and access, including a form of encryption, must be considered to protect information.

Another important factor in designing a good database for SQLite is the performance and the ability of the software to work efficiently and quickly among the operating system on a small device and app that has more demands on it today.

Testing both, manual and automatic, using products such as **Appium** for mobiles, is a must, because it can find out relevant bugs, issues, and problems, that manual testing may not have uncovered. The usage of SQLite in your application can be as complicated or as simple as you require, and the freedom and accessibility of code and experts are plentiful, to ensure that your app delivers what it sets out to achieve.

Summary

In this chapter, you learned how to design a database system for an application using SQLite. You learned the details of how to approach the design and outline certain concepts. The next chapter will show you how to administer an SQLite database and make use of this functionality.

3

Administering the Database

In this chapter, we are going to introduce you to administering the **SQLite** database and make you aware of the different components of this relational database system that best suits the mobile or tablet devices. SQLite is an embedded SQL engine and simply reads and writes to ordinary disk files instead of having a separate server process. It was designed for this purpose and is much easier to maintain and look after.

Apart from being a great database for programmers, SQLite is also an easier database to administer and maintain. There is no configuration or setup required to administer this database. It comes with a standard **command-line interface** (CLI) client that is available to administer the database(s).

There is a variety of languages that work with SQLite which are easier to maintain and add new functionality.

The following are the features of SQLite:

- SQLite is one of the most easy-to-learn databases, is easy to interact with, and gets on with the task of building a new database from scratch
- Its ability to integrate database engine itself into the code is a major boost for code development, performance, and interfacing
- It is easy to start, learn, perform, and get practical with how a relational database system, functions, glued together and is a store for your application's data

In the market, there are a variety of tools that can be used to make database administration on SQLite even easier to use, more practical to install and go and develop. In our case, only the **command-line program** (CLP) will be used.

These are some of the tools in the market:

- **RazorSQL**, located at `http://www.razorsql.com/features/sqlite_features.html`, is a tailored piece of software that works in a browser environment. It can highlight syntax and comes with an editor to write and update code, some visual administrator tools, and functionality unique to SQLite.

- Another tool is **SQLite Maestro,** located at `http://www.sqlmaestro.com/products/sqlite/maestro/`, which is a superior product aimed at the database management market for the creation, updation, and deletion of data using SQLite. For example, it includes a database designer, SQLite syntax checking, administrator tools, and a data exporter.

- **Navicat** is another database management tool for SQLite, located at `http://www.navicat.com/products/navicat-for-sqlite`. Their product comes with some good visual tools, database maintenance functionality, reporting, and data exporting, for example.

CLP is actually a separate program that has the SQLite engine compiled in it. CLP operates both as a command line tool and interactive shell. The command line mode is the facility **database administrators (DBAs)** can use to create tables for an application, upload data to the skeleton tables, and modify information so that it is ready for development, testing, and releasing. To start using the command, in terminal monitor, type `sqlite3`:

```
genedarochasMBP:AEM6 genedarocha$ sqlite3
SQLite version 3.8.5 2014-08-15 22:37:57
Enter ".help" for usage hints.
Connected to a transient in-memory database.
Use ".open FILENAME" to reopen on a persistent database.
sqlite>
```

If you type `sqlite3 <database name>`, the system will be loaded into the named database and will be ready to do work. For example, you can also type `sqlite3 -help`, as shown in the following screenshot, which will outline the commands available as part of the help. As shown in the following screenshot, there are a variety of options that will help the DBA or user perform tasks as required. Within `sqlite3`, to exit at the prompt, type `.exit` to leave the program. At the terminal prompt, `$`, type `sqlite3 -help` to get a list of commands, as shown here:

```
genedarochas-MacBook-Pro:AEM6 genedarocha$ sqlite3 —help
Usage: sqlite3 [OPTIONS] FILENAME [SQL]
FILENAME is the name of an SQLite database. A new database is created
if the file does not previously exist.
OPTIONS include:
   —bail                stop after hitting an error
   —batch               force batch I/O
   —column              set output mode to 'column'
   —cmd COMMAND         run "COMMAND" before reading stdin
   —csv                 set output mode to 'csv'
   —echo                print commands before execution
   —init FILENAME       read/process named file
   —[no]header          turn headers on or off
   —help                show this message
   —html                set output mode to HTML
   —interactive         force interactive I/O
   —line                set output mode to 'line'
   —list                set output mode to 'list'
   —mmap N              default mmap size set to N
   —nullvalue TEXT      set text string for NULL values. Default ''
   —separator SEP       set output field separator. Default: '|'
   —stats               print memory stats before each finalize
   —version             show SQLite version
   —vfs NAME            use NAME as the default VFS
genedarochas-MacBook-Pro:AEM6 genedarocha$ █
```

The preceding steps are manual and can be used by the database administrator. Shell scripts to automate database processes can ideally use the format, which can improve database performance.

Creating a database

To start, a database must be created. By using the following command to create the database, although it will be created, nothing will be physically stored in the database yet. There is no default place to store the SQLite database once it has been created. The location could be your home directory, a working directory, or a pre-created database directory:

```
$ sqlite3 testdatabase.db
```

By default, an environment is prepared ready effectively, for database objects, as defined by the preceding statement. SQLite was designed with the distinct policy of avoiding any size limits. To have a policy that would easily fit in the device's memory and be a 32-bit integer would work, but was not the best option. It proved to create problems since the product was pushed to extremes and the exploitation of security loopholes may have made the product vulnerable. The default settings of objects are generous and adequate for most applications. There are also different settings statements such as SQLITE_MAX_COLUMN that controls the maximum number of columns in a table, indexes, or view.

It is only when tables and indexes are created that the physical creation of the database actually starts. This allows the DBA to alter different page settings before the disk parameters and allocations are created. Thereafter, it is more difficult to change the settings.

Creating a table

To create a table in the new database, use the following commands:

```
Last login: Tue Jan 19 12:00:29 on ttys000
$ sqlite3
SQLite version 3.8.5 2014-08-15 22:37:57
Enter ".help" for usage hints.
Connected to a transient in-memory database.
Use ".open FILENAME" to reopen on a persistent database.
sqlite> create table temp (id integer primary key, name text,
address text);
sqlite>
```

After the preceding command is run to create a database, the create table temp statement is executed to make a temporary table. It has three columns, id which is a primary key whose value is automatically incremented; name, which is text; and address; which is also of text.

Inserting data

To insert data into the new table, use the following command. It is a simple operation to insert data into the table with the columns listed on the left-hand side, and the values and parameters, or data on the right-hand side of the same format type:

```
$ sqlite3
SQLite version 3.8.5 2014-08-15 22:37:57
Enter ".help" for usage hints.
Connected to a transient in-memory database.
Use ".open FILENAME" to reopen on a persistent database.
sqlite> insert into temp(name,address) values('Jon Smith','10
Downing Street London' );
sqlite>
```

Data is input into the `temp` table using data for two columns: `name` and `address`. Please note that no values are required for the `id` field since its value is provided internally by SQLite, which automatically increments its value.

Selecting data

To select data from the new table, follow the next command. It is a simple operation to fetch the information for display on the screen:

```
sqlite>
sqlite> .mode column
sqlite> .headers on
sqlite> select * from temp;
id          name        address
----------  ----------  ----------
1           Jon Smith
2           Bob Smith
sqlite>
```

Data is selected from the `temp` table using all columns, hence the character `*`, otherwise, a column name could have been specified instead, retrieving only that column data.

Creating an index

To create an index for the `temp` table, which will allow faster selection using the `id` field and also have a small overhead, which may be overtaken by the performance gain, use the following command:

```
$ sqlite3
SQLite version 3.8.5 2014-08-15 22:37:57
Enter ".help" for usage hints.
Connected to a transient in-memory database.
Use ".open FILENAME" to reopen on a persistent database.
sqlite> created index temp_idx on temp (name);
```

An index called `temp_idx` is created in the `name` column, which will allow faster access with a minimal overhead for data access.

Exporting data

To export data from SQLite, the .dump command is used, as shown in the following screenshot. No arguments are required and the complete database can be exported in this way. If an argument is added like a table name, then only their contents will be exported. By default, the .dump command will output the data to the screen. If you want to direct the output to a filesystem, use the .output statement plus a space, and then the file name, as shown in the following screenshot.

After the commands are used, a file is created in your current directory. To get back to outputting the data back to the screen, use the .output stdout command, as shown here.

Using these methods allows more flexibility, control, and better formatting output:

```
sqlite>
sqlite>
sqlite> .output temp.sql
sqlite> .dump
sqlite> .output stdout
sqlite>
```

As shown in the preceding screenshot, there is an output to the temp.sql file. The .dump command is issued to output all the information about the database to the temp.sql file. To put the output back to the screen, use the .output stdout command.

Viewing database schema data

SQLite offers several commands as part of a command set to get information about the contents of a database. For example, to get a list of tables, use the .table command. To find a specific table name, use a % symbol and text as a pattern to find the result, for example, .tables [pattern], as shown in the following screenshot. By issuing the .tables command and appending a %te% text to it, is a request to SQLite to list all its tables within the database that has the word te (in our case temp) in their name which are displayed correctly:

```
sqlite>
sqlite>
sqlite>
sqlite>
sqlite>
sqlite> .tables %te%
temp
sqlite>
```

Index data

Prior to the following example, a temp_idx index has been created, to get a list of indexes for the temp table, at the sqlite3 prompt .indices temp, which is actually the .indices command followed by the table name, as shown here:

```
sqlite>
sqlite> .indices temp
temp_idx
sqlite>
```

By using the preceding command, the temp table's index can be seen.

Schema data

To view the schema of the database, the following command can be issued, .schema, but type the .schema <table name> command to get specific information on a name database object. See the following screenshot for more information:

```
sqlite>
sqlite>
sqlite> .schema temp
CREATE TABLE temp(id integer primary key, name text, address text);
CREATE INDEX temp_idx on temp(id);
sqlite>
```

The preceding command shows the output from the temp set of tables and index from the database. The next command shows the whole database schema:

```
sqlite>
sqlite>
sqlite> .schema
CREATE TABLE temp(id integer primary key, name text, address text);
CREATE INDEX temp_idx on temp(id);
sqlite>
```

The SQLite master schema table shows tables and indexes that exist on the SQLite database.

Backing up the database

There are a couple of ways to back up your SQLite database. To make it portable, use the .dump statement as part of the CLP, which can export the entire database and scripts to the filesystem. An example can be seen as follows:

```
$ sqlite3 testdatabase.db .dump > temp.sql
```

The preceding statement shows how to invoke SQLite with a database name and pipe the output to a file called temp.sql.

Following is another way to invoke SQLite and then perform a backup interactively.

User can directly import the data, by the following set of commands:

```
sqlite>
sqlite> .output temp.sql
sqlite> .dump
sqlite> .output stdout
sqlite> .exit
```

The following command will open SQLite and the temp.db database, and import the temp.sql file to it. Within the temp.sql file, there will be scripts to read the source files and import data back to database (existing or new version):

```
$   sqlite3 temp.db < temp.sql
```

There is another way, just copy the temp.db file to a version called temp.backup, but the aforementioned methods are much better and portable, and there may be binary compatibility issues since SQLite does not have a great reputation for backward compatibility.

Database tools

There is a vast array of SQLite administration tools, and one of them is **SQL Browser** (http://sqlitebrowser.org/), which works on different platforms. Databases can be managed, tables can be exported or imported, and queries can be created, updated, and executed. The other tools are listed as follows:

* **RazorSQL**
* **Navicat**

- **SQL Maestro**
- **SQL Browser**
- **phpSQLiteAdmin**
- **SQLiteManager**
- **SQLite Expert**

Another previous or abandoned project for SQLite administration is **phpSQLiteAdmin**. This is now abandoned and the last update was in 2008. It is available at `http://phpsqliteadmin.sourceforge.net/`. phpSQLiteAdmin is a web interface for the administration of SQLite databases. It allows users to drop, create, and manage databases, and view database information like the schema, tables, indexes, and file metadata. There is a similar project in the market, namely; **Bitbucket** (available at `https://bitbucket.org/phpliteadmin/public/`).

SQLiteManager is a product that can manage databases to create, update, and import or export data; SQLiteManager is available at `http://www.sqlitemanager.org/`. This is a web-based administration tool for SQLite. Rows in the tables can be managed and user functions can be created as required. Again, this project and product is not active at present and there have been no updates since 2013. This product has now moved to Bitbucket and is no longer valid as SQLiteManager. However, since moving to Bitbucket in 2013, there have been no updates.

There is an additional tool, namely SQLite Expert (available at `http://www.sqliteexpert.com/`) that has a personal and a professional edition. For example, it has a built-in **SQL Query Builder**, facilities to import and export data, and data editing.

Database file information

The `sqlite_master` view outlines the details of all the database objects within SQLite. In SQLite, the maximum size for a database would be 2,147,483,646 pages at 65,536 bytes per page or 140,737,488,224,256 bytes (about 140 terabytes), While the minimum size for an SQLite database is a single 512-byte page. The best way to see which tables exist is by performing an SQL statement on the master table, as shown in the following set of commands:

```
sqlite> SELECT name FROM sqlite_master
   ...> WHERE type='table'
   ...> ORDER BY name;
temp
sqlite>
```

Effectively, download the `sqlite3_analyzer` program from the SQLite website. The program performs many functions, such as interrogating the database file and outputs a summary in text format showing the database structure, its environment, tables, indexes, the page sizes, entries, storage in bytes consumed, pages used, overflow pages, and unused bytes on primary pages.

The amount of detail available is impressive and useful when it comes to analyzing resources, components, and structure of a database.

The `sqlite3_analyzer` program can also be used in a variety of ways to use the statistics gained from using it. `sqlite3_analyzer` is a TCL script and is available at `http://www.sqlite.org/src/artifact/8e50b217c56a6a08`.

Summary

In this chapter, you learned how to administer and look after the SQLite relational database system, which has shown you in a simple way how to look after the database for your application. This chapter showed some of the basic elements of the SQLite database. It has covered the essentials of table creation and viewing tables that make up the schema. The topics are enough to get a grasp of the subject and master the basics. This chapter covers the basic elements and gave a helping hand to administer this easy-to-use database for mobile development. This chapter also summarizes how easy it is to administer as compared to other databases in the market. There are additional tools for SQLite Administration that can be found on the web. There are many more commands and not all have been shown as examples in this chapter. These are some of the methods of using and administering SQLite. This chapter showed you what is possible when you learn a few commands and how it can help use this simple, mobile database.

In the next chapter, you will learn all about the essentials of SQL. The chapter will outline how SQL can be used properly on this mobile database. It will show you how to use the SQLite method of using SQL compared to other databases and how easy it is to pick up SQL with SQLite.

4
Essentials of SQL

In this chapter, you will learn all about the essentials of SQL. It will outline what the major possibilities with SQL are and how it can be used properly on SQLite. SQL is fundamental to using SQLite and is mandatory for utilizing the benefits of SQL. It is relevant in many ways, because it is the way data is passed through, interrogated, and displayed, using variables.

We will discuss how the language is used with subclauses like "having", for example. Once you come to know and learn the essentials of how SQL is used in SQLite, it will make the whole subject easier.

SQL is also pronounced *sequel* in the industry and is the de facto standard for data retrieval using these commands and syntaxes. The instruction in this chapter will use a style and format that is easy to understand and follow. It makes use of the idea of replaying the code, repeating it, and remembering it well, for your knowledge and experience.

You will also see what data retrieval options and techniques are available to sort, collate, and order information as required. The examples shown in this chapter will provide easy-to-follow and useful instructions with advanced SQL commands. The results will be quick, or even instantaneous and can be practiced over and over again to gain the necessary knowledge. There will be tables such as `customers` or `salary` and different trigger names and SQL statements in this chapter.

The examples in this chapter will be ANSI compliant and should work with SQL databases such as SQLite, Oracle, Ingres, SQL Server, mySQL, MS Access, Informix, Sybase, and other ANSI SQL compliant databases. This chapter aims to give you that critical information, which will advance your skills as well. It will also act as a simple refresher and reminder of when you first learned them.

To start off, the SELECT statement is the easiest of the general commands, but it is also the core one of the pact. It allows the data inside the system to be visible by the end user in the choice of format and style requested, assuming it is syntactically correct.

There are many subcommands and clauses with the SELECT statement and some of those clauses are discussed in this chapter. The SELECT statement will have more focus due to its importance, and many options for data selection. As a developer or a DBA, it is always good to have the knowledge of possible options, which enable efficient queries to be written. This chapter will enable that knowledge and, for experts, refresh it. Although SQLite commands work and look the same for Oracle or MySQL, some of the SQLite ones are actually different.

Let's get started!

Transactions

A database **transaction** is a logical unit of work that contains several operations within. By definition, it will have four **ACID** properties: **atomic**, **consistent**, **isolated**, and **durable**.

A transaction must provide a sense of a full commitment to performing the work, or a way to rollback and not complete the work. It must also keep each transaction separate and isolated from the others, and ensure that transactions are completed, and information is written to the database. It must also reduce any amounts of database inconsistency and allow the best and proper way to recover from any failures.

Query plan

When a query is to be executed, a query plan is used by the database to forge a data path where the best and the most efficient types of routes are created. If there are table join, indexes, and a number of rows in the tables, a variety of mathematical calculations using different algorithms are prepared. Having an execution plan is useful when there are issues with SQL, and to debug multiple table joins and index setups, and follow a path to solve a data or programming issue.

Apart from the straightforward SQL statements in a plain format, there will be those statements that will be used within iOS and wrapped in one of the languages such as Objective-C or Swift.

When the query execution plan is executed, the data, the information, is geared for debugging only and should be used as guidance. Every SQLite release will have different updates that affect the product. The whole idea of a plan is to outline the strategy path an SQL command takes.

A keyword called **EXPLAIN**, or a phrase, namely, **EXPLAIN QUERY PLAN**, is required to be used for obtaining the details of a table. These commands are for debugging and analysis only. These commands are partially documented and the behavior is not always 100%:

```
sqlite> select * from salary
   ...> ;
1|Gene|32|London|10000.0
2|Sam|42|London|12000.0
3|Dan|22|New York|17000.0
4|Adam|28|New York|27000.0
sqlite>
sqlite> EXPLAIN SELECT * from Salary where Salary>=15000;
0|Init|0|15|0||00|
1|OpenRead|0|3|0|5|00|
2|Rewind|0|13|0||00|
3|Column|0|4|1||00|
4|RealAffinity|1|0|0||00|
5|Lt|2|12|1|(BINARY)|6d|
6|Rowid|0|3|0||00|
7|Column|0|1|4||00|
8|Column|0|2|5||00|
9|Column|0|3|6||00|
10|Copy|1|7|0||00|
11|ResultRow|3|5|0||00|
12|Next|0|3|0||01|
13|Close|0|0|0||00|
14|Halt|0|0|0||00|
15|Transaction|0|0|2|0|01|
16|TableLock|0|3|0|salary|00|
17|Integer|15000|2|0||00|
18|Goto|0|1|0||00|
sqlite>
```

Next, we see what an SQL statement with a `salary` selection will look like. Using the `EXPLAIN QUERY PLAN` command with the `SELECT` statement, the basic plan outlines the order of the table with its name. By learning the query execution plans effectively, you get a view of how SQLite accesses your data and see how it is committed:

```
sqlite> EXPLAIN QUERY PLAN SELECT * FROM Salary where Salary >=20000;
0|0|0|SCAN TABLE Salary
```

The `EXPLAIN QUERY PLAN` command exists as a guidance and plan for executing the SQL Query. It will report and provide information that relates to how the database indices are effectively used to access the data.

The **system catalog** is also the master place where all tables and indexes are listed. For example, the `sqlite_master` table is the, as shown here:

```
sqlite>
sqlite>
sqlite> select type,name from sqlite_master;
table|salary
sqlite>
```

SQL basics

SQLite also has some other features for using SQL, such as finding the greatest `id` from a column, and also the last insert and its `id`, as shown in the following:

```
sqlite>
sqlite> select max(id) from temp;
3
sqlite>
sqlite> select last_insert_rowid();
3
sqlite>
```

Insert with a subselect clause

The `INSERT` statement is the one used to add data into the database. However, the example to date has only shown data from fixed information or program variables. There is another way to insert data, which comes from another table based on the select criteria and data/column matching. This is an insert with a **subselect** clause; see the following example:

```
SQLite> Insert into Salary values (Select id, name, salary from
salary_import where name='Smith');

SQLite> Select * from Salary where name like '%smith%';
```

There are several variations available on the format, as shown in the preceding example. The SQL is flexible and there are options to select different data and offer computations on the last row of IDs.

Update with a subselect clause

As discussed in the previous chapters, the UPDATE statement is used to change existing data in a table from variables in a program or from fixed data. However, there is another way to update data to the destination table from a source table where there is a match and link, as shown in the following. The UPDATE statement will modify more than one column. The Where clause will identify which column(s) are to be updated. This is one of the simplest and easiest SQL commands to understand:

```
SQLite> Update salary = 15000
Where name='John Smith';

SQLite> Select * from Salary where name like '%smith%';
```

Select with a subselect clause

As discussed in the previous chapters, the SELECT statement is used to retrieve and display information from the core of the database to the user. The SELECT statement is a very popular and powerful command with a variety of options and choices to retrieve the data. A **subselect** or **subquery** is a nested piece of SQL within the original SQL, that is embedded near a WHERE clause. The subquery or subselect will only be used to retrieve information that links up to the main select query using the specific column names.

These subselect clauses can be used within the DELETE, INSERT, UPDATE, and SELECT SQL commands, with operators such as =, <, >, >=, <=, IN, or BETWEEN, for example. There are some rules that apply to subqueries, for example, the subcommand must only have one column in the SELECT clause, unless multiple columns are selected in the main SQL statement.

The subselect queries must use parentheses as part of their syntax, to outline the subquery itself. The main part of the query can have the ORDER BY syntax, but it cannot be in the subquery. If multiple rows are returned using these types of queries, then operators such as IN must be used. The BETWEEN word can be used in a subquery as long as it is not the BETWEEN operator itself:

```
sqlite> SELECT * FROM PERSONNEL WHERE ID IN (SELECT ID FROM SALARY
WHERE SALARY > 15000);
```

Data integrity

Data integrity is very important in maintaining how tables and data relationships are defined and protected. There are four types of integrity: user defined, referential, entity, and domain.

The mastering of data manipulation, database design, development, and administration is key to ensure that applications built using SQLite perform well, and are kept free from data crashes, data corruptions, and security issues.

When a column's datatype is set, it is a form of data integrity. Data integrity can be enhanced by only allowing certain values.

When a mechanism is designed to maintain the primary keys in a table by a unique tuple or row identifier, it is known as entity integrity.

Referential integrity occurs when, for example, two tables are linked by a common column datatype and no new data can be added to one table without being added to the second. Referential integrity ensures that data is cleaned and linked properly.

Default values

The **default values** for columns is valuable because it enforces data integrity and ensures that a value is entered on the database. It also means that some SQL statements are smaller than others. A standard type of statement without its column being added is an id field, where the primary key is defined, and when an INSERT statement is used, the id field is not required, as shown in the following.

The DBA can create columns to store current_timestamp in the database automatically, which is good for logging and time stamping.

```
sqlite> INSERT into salary (name, salary, bonus) values ('John
Smith',15000,2000); sqlite> SELECT * FROM salary;

id          name        salary      bonus
-----       --------    ---------   --------
1           Peter Jones 10000       3000
2           Sam Smith   15000       1000
3           John Smith  15000       2000
```

Constraint checking

To ensure that the right data is inputted into columns on a table, certain rules are imposed, and these are called constraints. These rules enforce data accuracy, limit corruption, and format issues and data reliability are increased and maintained.

At table level, it will apply to the whole table, but at column level, it will apply only to one certain column level. How they can be used is given as follows:

- The .UNIQUE constraint will make sure column data information is not the same

- The .PRIMARY key, each data row in the table is identified in SQLite

- .NOT NULL makes sure that no column has a NULL value stored

- DEFAULT will sets up a default value, when no value is specified or entered

Foreign keys

When two or more tables need to link together on a common column, it is known as a **referencing key** or **foreign key**. SQLite supports relation integrity and supports foreign key constraints, like other databases. It is usually designed by the DBA and involves a column ID, for example, to match an ID on the second or third table.

There must be a logical reference between the table columns and actual data for it to perform well. SQLite will use the foreign key as part of the create table statement; an example is shown in the following:

```
CREATE Table Salary (
id integer primary key,
name text,
salary
};
```

Updating Views

A **VIEW** is a command that can use a combination of tables and joins to show the user or program a set of predefined data, as required. Effectively, it gives you a view of the data. You cannot DELETE, UPDATE, or INSERT from a view.

As a view is defined with a specific name, which is stored in the database, it can be effectively referenced as a table to another SQL statement, as part of a statement to be manipulated.

If a keyword such as Temporary or Temp exists within the create and view words, then that view is only seen by that database connection and is removed upon the connection closing, hence the temp/temporary name.

If a database name is referenced when the view is created, it will reside within that specific database.

Index use

After a table is created with its column and datatypes, it is almost ready to use. The primary columns for data linking are done, but it is not quite ready as defined by a DBA. Instead, an index can be created to speed up SQL queries and act as special lookup tables that SQLite will use as a way of getting information faster.

An **index** has a data pointer, which will quickly reference the data and bring it back, thus making access quicker without much overhead generally. By definition, indexes do have an overhead in their own right, but the overheads of the index are dwarfed by the performance and efficiency gained. This could be useful for mobile applications because of their limited resource and network access.

A database index as an example is similar to the one located in a book, where you can find what you want because you know what it is, and just opens the book to right page, after reading the index.

The index is slow on data input but fast on the SELECT queries, with or without the WHERE clause. Once an index is created, it can also be dropped without affecting the core data of a table. The following is a simple example of an index called table_index_name being created on the customer table:

```
CREATE INDEX table_index_name ON customer;
```

A second example shows how an index is created to reference a column called salary, which is used multiple times in many queries:

```
CREATE INDEX table_index_salary ON customer (salary);
```

Here, an index will speed up access. An index called table_index_salary is created on the customer table, which is created on the salary column.

There are also indexes called **composite indexes**, which actually index more than one column on a database for further performance gains, but also an overhead on data input. As shown in the following, an index is created and is linked to two columns: salary and bonus. Rather than having two indexes with more overhead issues, a composite index maybe better, since it is one index with a reference to two columns:

```
CREATE INDEX table_index_salary ON customer (salary, bonus);
```

When creating indexes, the database server will also create implicit indexes that are automatic. If, as a DBA, you wish to see them, use the following example:

```
sqlite> .indices customer;
```

Triggers

Triggers are an efficient way of using SQL commands to interact efficiently with the database. They are quick, and are embedded within the create `trigger` command.

A trigger is made up of a trigger name, references to the tables involved, an event of time (like before, or after value changes), the type of operation (like insert, update, or delete), with a variety of tables and columns to complete the operation.

The syntax has to be right and the tests should ensure that the updates and changes are correct to ensure data concurrency and stability with no corruptions.

This trigger is called `update_customer_trigger`, which performs an UPDATE query on the `customers` table. The update is going to affect the `tel_no` column. So, the current telephone column `tel_no` is going to be updated, where it will equal the value from the new table, and its column `tel_no` − (`tel_no` = `new.tel_no`), where the link of customer name (`customer_name`), equals the `old.name` column.

Updated triggers must use specific columns for a table, which are predefined, unlike the `insert` or `delete` ones

```
sqlite> select sql from sqlite_master where name='update_customer_
trigger';

CREATE TRIGGER update_customer_trigger UPDATE OF tel_no ON customers
BEGIN      UPDATE orders SET tel_no = new.tel_no WHERE customer_name =
old.name;    END
```

Synchronous writes

Synchronous writes are part of the SQL engine, which will ensure that data changes are written to the disk area, as required, for transaction reasons and the way databases work. In the case of SQLite, these operate under different statuses or settings of NORMAL, FULL, or OFF. For performance reasons, SQLite commits can be switched off by the DBA as required.

The OFF setting carries on its tasks quickly without much slowing down, minimal interruptions, and increased performance. However, in the case of a database crash, the data integrity will remain okay, but in the case of system crash and power loss, there is a good chance that corruption of the database itself may occur. There are performance gains to be made, but there are also risks associated with this move.

The FULL setting has to ensure that data is saved to disk properly and in good time before carrying on. This method is not good for performance, but is the most robust and the safest. If there are data corruptions or system crashes, users can be assured that no database corruption will occur.

The NORMAL setting will slow down at intervals to protect the data and commit transactions to disk. A database crash or a power failure could damage the database, but a more serious hardware error could be worse.

Database locking and deadlocks

A **deadlock** occurs when one or many actions or SQL statements compete for data access and table updates or manipulation at the same time as another process or action. Since it works with a transaction, one process can't move forward or complete because the other process or action holds, and is waiting for a resource, hence a deadlock.

So, in a database, records of process one would attempt to update, but process two would like to update some of the same rows, or a conflict of another table in which the transaction occurs. Some form of data locking mechanism to manage and reduce conflict must happen. Code around the transaction can be added with a retry indicator of three, for example, so if there is a deadlock, it will retry, and after the third attempt, it would roll back or give the user an opportunity to retry.

Deadlocking is a common occurrence in multithreaded and multiprocessing operating systems, which are performing a variety of tasks and attempting to complete with positive results.

See the following example on how SQL transactions will end up in a deadlock. In this case, both transactions/sessions will be in a deadlock state. **Session 2** will try to insert/write to the database and create a locking to get exclusive rights to protect, and ensure it can insert the record without any problem. **Session 1** tries to write as well, which also causes a deadlock situation. Effectively, we have a situation where **Session 1** and **Session 2** do not want to lose access or control until the other leaves, which lets the deadlock continue, as shown here:

Session 1	Session 2
sqlite3>	sqlite3>
	sqlite3>insert into temp(name,address) values('Gene','London');
sqlite3> select * from temp;	
	sqlite3> commit;

Session 1	Session 2
	SQL Error Message: database locked
sqlite3> insert into temp(name,address) values('Gene','London');	
SQL Error Message: database locked	

FMDB SQLite wrapper

In addition to using standard SQL, the FMDB SQLite wrapper, written in Objective-C, can be of assistance to those who prefer an alternative and easier way to work with SQLite.

For more information on the FMDB specification and code examples, refer to `https://github.com/ccgus/fmdb`.

There are three main classes in FMDB:

- **FMDatabase**: This is the single SQLite database that executes your SQL statements
- **FMResultSet**: This will hold and display the output and results from the FMDatabase
- **FMDatabaseQueue**: This will enable you to update and use many threads within this class if you want to perform queries and updates on multiple threads

Database creation and opening

The database is defined and allocated to a location and directory:

```
FMDatabase *db = [FMDatabase databaseWithPath:@"/tmp/atmp.db"];
```

To engage with the database, you must connect and open it up, as shown in the following:

```
if (![db open]) {      [db release];      return; }
```

SQL in iOS

To select data, methods like executeQuery can be used to return the FMResultSet object if successful, or 0 upon failure. There are methods, such as lastErrorMessage or lastErrorcode, to find out if the query has worked or failed:

```
FMResultSet *s = [db executeQuery:@"SELECT * FROM aTable"]; while ([s
next]) {     //retrieve values for each record }
```

For multiple rows, [FMResultSet next] must be used to see or read the values returned from the query, even if the recordset is one, for example.

The following command shows how to use FMResultSet to select multiple queries as required:

```
FMResultSet *s = [db executeQuery:@"SELECT COUNT(*) FROM aTable"]; if
([s next]) {     int totalCount = [s intForColumnIndex:0]; }
```

FrmresultSet offers several methods to the programmer to retrieve; some examples are as follows:

- intForColumn:
- longForColumn:
- longLongIntForColumn:

Some of the aforementioned methods by default will have the {type} ForColumnIndex: variant, which will be used to get the data based on the position of the column in the rows and not the name itself.

The preceding code using FMDatabase comes from GitHub and is the standard code used for these types of operations. It has been used to improve the ease of interacting with SQLite, instead of the conventional standard method.

Summary

In this chapter, you learned about the essentials of SQL in relation to the SQLite database, and also what you need to be aware of, and the knowledge required, to build SQL statements and interactions with SQLite and iOS as a basic start.

In the next chapter, you will learn all about exposing the C API, its impact and uses within IOS, and how it works as part of SQLite. The next chapter will also mention how the C API is at the core of SQLite and how it is used.

5
Exposing the C API

In this chapter, you will learn all about the **C API** (**C application programming interface**) and, through code, make use of it in your application. By having over 200 API calls to this light, small, and expanding API set, SQLite will surprise you with how it can achieve what you want from a mobile and flexible database.

You will look at some of the syntax and usage and see how to actually extend the functionality of SQLite by using its vast arsenal of API calls.

SQLite C components' functionality

SQLite has been written using C language, and its creator has enabled it to be exposed and has enhanced its functionality by having an API, the C API. In general, SQLite has many different API calls, for example, about 200 APIs for different functionalities. As a programmer, you may find it hard to accept, but the APIs are designed for specific tasks, for example, the `sqlite3_reset()` function clears the object connected with the SQLite prepared statement and resets it to its original state and value.

To start with, the two core objects are the database connection and the prepared statement objects. The order and the types of functions give you an idea of how to write an SQL transaction to connect to a database, create a table and an index, and populate it with an `insert` statement. These functions form the main elements of the SQL-C interface functions, allowing data to be connected and passed from code to SQLite.

sqlite3_open()

The `sqlite3_open(const char *filename, sqlite ** Db_name)` will open a connection to the SQLite database file at your chosen location and return the database connection object, which will be used by other SQLite components or functions.

The sqlite3_open() function is required to make a connection before any other operation can take place. It will enable the rest of the operations to follow.

If, in the sqlite3_open function, the filename does not contain a NULL, the function will use a value from the provided values, or if no database file already exists, SQLite will attempt to open a new database using the name. Once a database connection via the sqlite_open() function had been achieved, commands such as sqlite_prepare() can go forward. An example of sqlite3_open() is shown here:

```
sqlite3 *thedb;
int recordcounter  = sqlite3_open("test.db", &thedb);
```

sqlite3_prepare()

With a new database connection, we will get a pointer address that will serve as the input for the sqlite_prepare() command. The statements will compile the source SQL statements into the object code. The functionality of the sqlite3_prepare() function is to bind and set up the relevant parameters to link up your query strings as part of the data process. Here is a brief example outlining the process for sqlite3_prepare():

```
sqlite3_stmt        *a_statement

NSString *insertSQL = [NSString stringWithFormat: @"INSERT INTO TEMP (name, address) VALUES (\"%@\", \"%@\")",
  name.text, address.text];

const char *insert_statement = [insertSQL UTF8String];

recordcounter = sqlite3_prepare_v2(thedb, insert_statement, -1, &a_statement, 0);
```

sqlite3_step()

The sqlite3_step() statement will analyze, inspect, and evaluate the output object code from the previous the sqlite3_prepare() statement. It will execute a prepare statement and will return an SQLite status code. If there is data, then the SQLITE_ROW status code will be returned. When the statement has finished executing, the SQLITE_DONE status code will be returned. Any other returned value will be regarded as an error. SQLite3_step() must be reset for it to be used again.

This method is mainly used for the SELECT statement. Other statements such as DELETE, UPDATE, or INSERT will execute to completion from the first record to the last:

```
sqlite3_stmt        *a_statement

recordcounter = sqlite3_prepare_v2(thedb, insert_statement, -1, &a_statement, 0);

if (sqlite3_step(a_statement) == SQLITE_DONE)
{
        return YES;
}
else
    {    NSLog(@"Failed");
}
```

sqlite3_column()

As the SQLITE3_prepare statement is being evaluated, the SQLITE3_column statement displays a single column as part of the result set. SQLITE3_column performs a placeholder function within the SQLITE API and is the centerpoint for a variety of other functions, such as SQLite_column_count().

See the following for more information:

```
sqlite3_stmt        *a_statement

recordcounter = sqlite3_prepare_v2(thedb, insert_statement, -1, &a_statement, 0);

if (sqlite3_step(a_statement) == SQLITE_DONE)
{
        return YES;
}
else
    {    NSLog(@"Failed");
}

int a_step = sqlite3_step(a_statement);

if (a_step == SQLITE3_ROW) {
    printf("%s: ",sqlite3_column_text(res,0));
    printf("%s: ",sqlite3_column_text(res,1));  }
```

sqlite3_finalize()

As the name suggests, this statement will finalize and seal all prepared statements. Once the `sqlite3_finalize` statement has been executed, any memory is deallocated and internal process resources are released. Once completed, the statement cannot be reused and is not valid internally. See the following command for more information:

```
sqlite3_finalize(a_statement);
```

sqlite3_close()

This is the last component to be executed, namely the `sqlite3_close` command, which will close the database using the pointer and reference from the database connection, and previously created prepared statements will have to be finished before the connection is closed.

As mentioned previously, in order to call or run SQL statements within SQLite or any other database, you must connect to the database and once you finish your work, you must disconnect.

The preceding `SQLite_open()` statement is a way of using the C API directly without any implementation of the Swift language. The following are two methods for using the open database statement, in C API and in Swift. There are two types of approach:

- Using the **C API** with the open database statement
- Using Swift with the open database statement

Using the C API with the open database statement

Have a look at the following code:

```
var db1 = SQLiteDatabase();
db1.open("/path/to/database1.sqlite");
```

A variable of `db1` is defined to call the `SQLiteDatabase()` function. Then the `db1.open()` method is used with the data within the brackets to point to the `database1` database, as shown in the preceding code.

Using Swift with the open database statement

An alternative way to open the database using Swift is as follows:

```
let datadocuments = NSSearchPathForDirectoriesInDomains(.
DocumentDirectory,
.UserDomainMask, true)[0] as String

let databasepath = documents.stringByAppendingPathComponent("tester.
sqlite")

// open the database

var databasedb: DBPointer = nil

if sqlite3_open(path, &databasedb) != SQLITE_OK
{
    println("error opening database")
}
```

Remember that for Swift, you have to import the `sqlite3.h` file and add the `libsqlite3.0.dylib` SQLite library to your project.

To add this `libsqlite3.0.dylib` to your project, follow these steps:

1. Select the target and framework within the project editor.
2. Click on **Build Phases** at the top of the editor and open the link with the libraries section.

3. Click on **+** to add the framework or, in our case, the `libsqlite3.0.dylib` SQLite library.

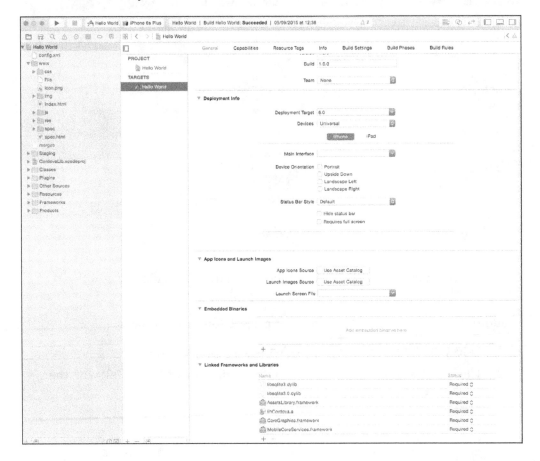

4. A search `NSSearchPAthForDirectoriesinDomains` is used to set up the `datadocuments` variable, and then the `databasepath` variable is set up as a place for the `sqlite` file.

5. A variable of `databasedb` is set up and a check is performed to see if the `sqlite3_open()` function with the input parameters actually works to open the database, otherwise an error message is shown.

The beauty of SQLite is its flexibility and the extensions of the product, which include extendable SQL features such as collating sequences, and SQL functions that enable your application to be different and unique. The range of change and ability to extend the app is growing.

The extension you build can be linked to your app and you can use of a function such as `SQLite_extension_init` as a pointer or address to ensure names don't conflict.

The SQLite extension is classed as a **DLL** (a **dynamic link library** — a collection of programs that are used when required by larger applications).

DLLs by definition require an entry or starting point to engage with a program. It is where processes attach themselves to the DLL and a join or connection is made to exchange information and use functionality. The entry point function is used to perform cleanup tasks or initialization when engaged. When a process uses the entry point function, it can be used for allocating memory or virtual address space.

SQLite can use load extensions, which are coded outside SQLite and tested and deployed as necessary. Once developed, these extensions can easily link up to SQLite. If there was some functionality SQLite did not have, a third party could develop it and make it available to potential customers or users in a particular industry, for example.

When creating an extension for SQLite, the extension differs for each operating system:

- Some Unix systems use the `.so` file extension
- Windows systems use the `.dll` extension
- OS X (Mac) systems use the `.Dylib` extension

This shows the great flexibility of the software, which can cater to a variety of operating systems and, therefore, allow the SQLite database to be applied to different systems and technologies.

load_extension()

The `load_extension(X,Y)` function is another capable function that allows functions/extensions to be loaded. Its methods are similar to that of the `sqlite3_load_extension()` C interface. Both these methods use entry points, and a name is required as an identifier. Null pointers can be passed in for the input argument.

There are commands that change the database and don't return any results, such as the `Update` statement. The function that carries out this task is `sqlite3_exec()`. This method is faster and is not difficult to learn or execute.

sqlite3_exec()

The `sqlite3_exec()` process has a pointer to an open database, a single or a list of SQL statements using a pointer to the callback function as part of its functionality. It will use one or several SQL statements combined with a null-terminated string for processing. Each row of the query will have a pointer to a callback function. There will also be a pointer sent ahead as part of the first argument to a callback function. A pointer to an error string variable is included.

sqlite3_config()

The functionality of `sqlite3_config()` is useful for allowing changes to be made at a global level. The `sqlite3_config()` must be called before opening the database. The `sqlite3_config()` interface will allow SQLite's memory allocation to be adjusted, producing an error log for the whole process. It sets up and configures the SQLite library, controlling many aspects of memory allocation and related resources.

To extend SQLite, further functions and routines such as `sqlite3_create_collation()`, `sqlite3_create_function()`, `sqlite3_create_module()`, and `sqlite3_vfs_register()` are investigated and used as necessary to improve the product functionality. Maintenance of these systems will be limited to those who know and use the technology.

The following is an example of using some of the database functions using the `select`, `update`, `delete`, and `insert` commands with Apple's new language, Swift.

As mentioned previously, there are different SQLite wrappers out there, some specifically written for Swift (not many), but the most common one is **FMDB**, which has been tested for different apps:

1. In order to bring Objective-C into Swift, a "bridging header" is required, namely `sqlite3.h`. To use this header, use the following command:

   ```
   #import <sqlite3.h>
   ```

2. Add the `libsqlite3.0.dylib` SQLite library to your project, as discussed previously.

3. Once the `libsqlite3.0.dylib` library has been added to the project, the next task is to create the database.

4. Next, use the `sqlite3_exec` functionality to perform the `create table...` SQL statement, for example, as part of using Swift:

   ```
   if sqlite3_exec(databasedb,
     "create table if not exists test table (id integer
     primary key autoincrement, name2 text)", nil, nil, nil)
     != SQLITE_OK {
   ```

```
let errmsg = String.fromCString(sqlite3_errmsg(db))

println("error creating new table: \(errmsg)") }
```

5. The next statement to use is an `Insert` statement to enter data into the newly created `test` table. The following information will show how to prepare, bind, and step the SQL statement. The `sqlite3_prepare_v2` function will be used to prepare the SQL using a placeholder of `?` to bind the required value:

```
var statement: DBPointer = nil
if sqlite3_prepare_v2(databasedb, "insert into test (name)
  values (?)", -1, &statement, nil) != SQLITE_OK
{
    let errmsg = String.fromCString(sqlite3_errmsg(databasedb))
        println("error preparing insert: \(errmsg)")
}

if sqlite3_bind_text(statement, 1, "data", -1,
  SQLITE_TRANSIENT) != SQLITE_OK
{
    let errmsg = String.fromCString(sqlite3_errmsg(databasedb))
    println("failure binding record data: \(errmsg)") }

if sqlite3_step(statement) != SQLITE_DONE
{
    let errmsg = String.fromCString(sqlite3_errmsg(databasedb))
    println("failure inserting record data: \(errmsg)") }
```

6. A constant, `SQLITE_TRANSIENT`, can be used as a part of the following process:

```
let SQLITE_STATIC =
  sqlite3_destructor_type(DBPointer(bitPattern: 0))
let SQLITE_TRANSIENT =
  sqlite3_destructor_type(DBPointer(bitPattern: -1))
```

This is the standard way of using these variables. Sometimes these variables don't work if they have not been included as part of the `.h` file or as defined in the following section. They are not supported in Swift because of "unsafe pointer casting."

The prepare statement

As part of the prepare statement, the functionality of sqlite3_prepare_v2 is used with the SQL statement, using the question mark (?) as a placeholder to bind input values. This is shown in the following example:

```
var statement: DBPointer = nil
if sqlite3_prepare_v2(databasedb, "insert into testtable (name)
  values (?)", -1, &statement, nil) != SQLITE_OK
{
    let errmsg = String.fromCString(sqlite3_errmsg(db))
      println("error preparing the insert: \(errmsg)")
}
if sqlite3_bind_text(statement, 1, "Bind1", -1, SQLITE_TRANSIENT)
  != SQLITE_OK
{
    let errmsg = String.fromCString(sqlite3_errmsg(db))
      println("failure binding this statement: \(errmsg)")
}
if sqlite3_step(statement) != SQLITE_DONE

{

    let errmsg = String.fromCString(sqlite3_errmsg(db))
      println("failure on inserting data : \(errmsg)") }
```

The standard was of using the SQLITE_STATIC and SQLITE_TRANSIENT as setup is as follows:

```
#define SQLITE_STATIC((sqlite3_destructor_type)0)
#define SQLITE_TRANSIENT((sqlite3_destructor_type)-1)4
```

In Swift 2, the code could change, as shown in the following:

```
"Internal let SQLITE_STATIC = unsafeBitCast(0,
  sqlite3_destructor_type.self) internal let SQLITE_TRANSIENT =
  unsafeBitCast(-1, sqlite3_destructor_type.self)"
```

Next, let's perform an insert statement using a NULL value to prove that SQL does work:

```
if sqlite3_reset(statement) != SQLITE_OK
{
    let errmsg = String.fromCString(sqlite3_errmsg(databasedb))

    println("error resetting prepared statement: \(errmsg)")
}

if sqlite3_bind_null(statement, 1) != SQLITE_OK
```

```
{
    let errmsg = String.fromCString(sqlite3_errmsg(databasedb))

    println("failure binding the null value: \(errmsg)")
}

if sqlite3_step(statement) != SQLITE_DONE
{
    let errmsg = String.fromCString(sqlite3_errmsg(databasedb))

    println("failure inserting null: \(errmsg)")
}
```

As mentioned previously, SQLite can work by allowing each SQL statement to be prepared once, evaluated, executed, and then destroyed, but it also has the facility to prepare the same system and be evaluated several different times by using the routines like the `sqlite3_reset()` and `sqlite3_bind()` functions. SQLite is a good and functional database that would work for different applications without any adjustments.

The following code is then used to close the database after the work has been done:

```
if sqlite3_close(databasedb) != SQLITE_OK

{

    println("error closing the database")

}databasedb = nil
```

This is the advantage of the language having built-in SQL functionality.

The information in this chapter has focused on the functionality of the C API. Developers today will extend and use different types of functionalities, as required, for their apps, but embedding the use of Swift, Objective-C, Java, or other languages.

Summary

In this chapter, you learned how to extend the C API and produce code, which can be used to build some interesting, exciting, new, and intelligent data-driven applications and promote the use of SQLite. The language used is Swift. In the next chapter, you will learn briefly how to use Swift with IOS and SQLite, and you will be shown how to install Xcode and work with Swift and an SQLite library.

6

Using Swift with iOS and SQLite

In this chapter, you will look at using the new programming language from Apple called **Swift**. It is a new language created by Apple and has very powerful features to perform a variety of tasks and is now open source. Apple released it, and it has grown so fast that in the months and years to come, it will be the de facto standard for coding using Apple devices. You will see how Swift works with iOS, Xcode, and SQLite.

It has been an extraordinary journey since Swift was announced at the WWDC 2014 in San Francisco. In 2015, Apple announced that Swift would be open source. The language itself allows you to write high-level code and even low-level code with ease. It is a culmination of languages, such as Python, C, and Objective-C, making it faster and easier, and it's available on a number of platforms.

Can you imagine what is going to happen in the next few years? Design patterns and skills are developing at a fast rate, and applications will be rewritten and deployed using the new language.

We will show you how to install Xcode to work with Swift and any SQLite libraries. There will be a few examples of how to get the new language to work with SQLite and Xcode. The examples and information given in this chapter will allow you, as a beginner, to get to grips with learning this new language and gaining new skills.

Basic requirements

All f#Apple development is completed on a Mac. You will require the following:

- A MAC computer with the Maverick or Yosemite operating system
- The Xcode application development environment
- A good understanding of object-oriented programming
- A basic understanding of the Swift language, from the Swift reference guide

 For reference information, you can check out the *Apple Developer Guide* at `https://developer.apple.com/library/ios/navigation/#section=Resource%20Types&topic=Guides`. A positive attitude to learning and developing your skills is very important.

Starting an Xcode Project with Swift

Xcode has been impacted with release fixes and enhances to the Swift language. So, sometimes, code that used to work easily now requires some coding changes before the compiler is happy with it. This is something that will always happen with a changing code base for a new language.

Start by opening Xcode. The best version of Xcode is the latest one, available from the Apple App Store at `https://developer.apple.com/xcode/download/`. Install Xcode, and when everything is set up, launch Xcode and follow these steps:

1. Create a new project (*Cmd+Shift+N*).
2. In the template selector, make sure **iOS | Application** is selected. Choose the **Single View Application** template to start the process:

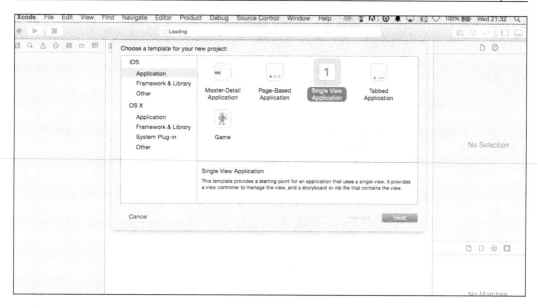

3. You are then prompted to add the project name, so add a name like `Test Swift Project`.

4. Next, add in the company name as `Voxstar Ltd` or your company's name.

5. Next, add in the organizer identifier, in our case `com.voxstar. testswiftproject`, which will identify a name for your apps and that is how it will be recognized by Apple.

6. Next, for the computer language, select Swift instead of Objective-C, which is what we are using in this chapter.

7. For the devices, select **iPhone**, also ensure that the **Use Core Data** option is not selected. See the following screenshot as an example:

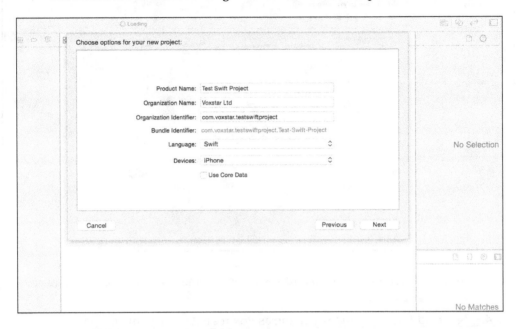

8. Click on the **Next** button to continue this process. Thereafter, you have to store the location of your project files; we suggest you use the location where the main .swift directory is stored, as shown in the following screenshot. For this example, use the Documents directory, select and click on **Next**, and a new directory called Test Swift App will be created. The following screenshots show the directory and project information within:

9. Once the **Create** button is clicked on, the project details page is displayed, as shown in the following screenshot. A set of standard files, templates, and components are used as part of Xcode:

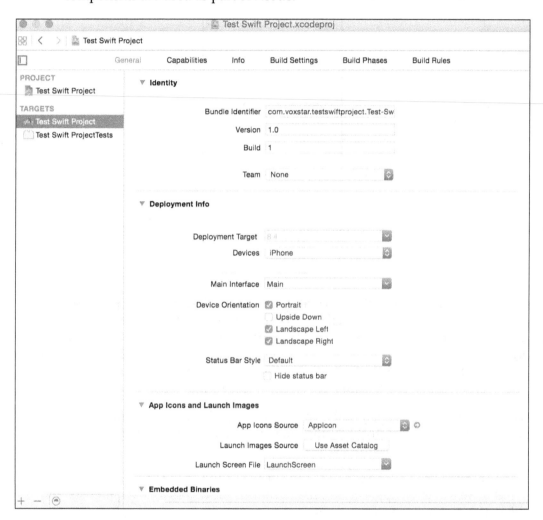

10. To show what the standard app using an iPhone would look like, click on the Play button and watch the default screen and the output from the iPhone 6 simulator:

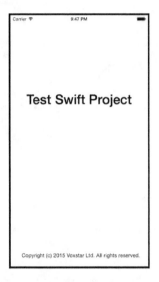

However, the first main entry place for the Swift application is the `AppDelegate.swift` file. This file is located in the application directory. Under the application directory, there will be a directory with the name of the app, and this is where the `AppDelegate.swift` file is located. In Xcode, click on it to open and you will find an array of information. This information will start with the standard comments that use your name and company details as part of the setup.

The main piece of information thereafter is the `import UIKit` statement. If you have developed in Objective-C before, this statement will be obvious and very familiar and reconcilable.

The UIKit will provide the essential infrastructure and backbone to manage and build these iOS Swift applications. It will contain the necessary user interface and other architecture to even handle and interact with the rest of the app. It provides support for motion-based events and handling touch events as well.

It will also support a model for iCloud support in addition to handling web and text content. It will support Apple and a push notification service. Further information can be obtained from the Developer Apple site:

Unlike Objective-C or other standard programming languages, Swift does not have a main function or file. Instead, you just mention the @UIApplicationMain statement in the main Swift file and all the relevant components are included. This line of code may never need to change, unless there is a major update or change.

Using the SQLite 3 Library

Before starting to code, you must add a specific library for SQLite. Within Xcode, ensure that the **General** tab is selected and visible. At the end of the page, look out for the **Linked Frameworks and Libraries** section. View and click on the icon with the plus sign, as shown in the following screenshot:

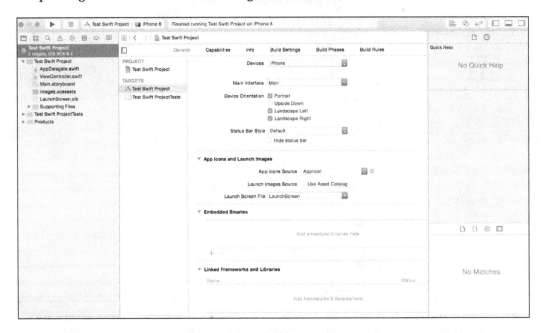

A modal window will appear; please enter the word `sqlite`, and from the list of information, select the **libsqlite3.dylib** option, as shown in the following screenshot:

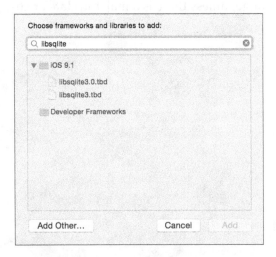

After selecting it, click on the **Add** button to move forward.

As part of this chapter, we will use **FMDB** and an Objective-C wrapper around SQLite to show the database SQLite with Swift. **FMDB** stands for **Flying Meat Database**, and it easily interacts with SQLite and actually saves time and effort. For example, the FMDB will be linked to one SQLite database and will be there for the execution of SQL queries. The output is FMResultsSet, which shows results for queries executed on the FMDB.

 The class of FMDatabaseQueue is there to handle updates, queries, and multiple threading.

The FMDB approach with an application that performs the SQL commands of Insert, Select, Delete, and Update will be used on a table called Mortgage. The Mortgage table will have a **Name** field and a **Mortgage Roll Number** field for the account details, as a very simple example.

The following is a screenshot of the actual user design using the View controller scene tool within Xcode to create the basic screen layout. This will outline and show the resulting action to be followed and executed when a button is clicked:

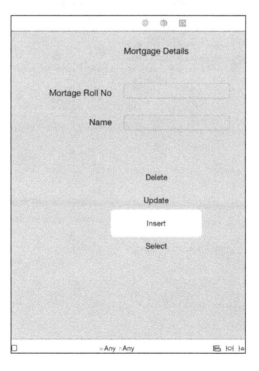

There are many tools to manage the SQLite database, and one of these is the **SQLite Manager Add-on** in the Firefox browser, to administer the database. The add-on can be obtained from `https://addons.mozilla.org/en-US/firefox/addon/sqlite-manager/`.

The add-on product has some of the following features for administrators:

- Manage the SQLite database on your machine
- Get a tree view of database objects
- There are easy and helpful dialogs that are easy to manage as well, for example, triggers, views, and tables
- A platform to execute SQL queries
- Export tables or views in UTF-8/UTF-16
- It is also possible to execute multiple SQL statements in the **Execute** tab

Open Firefox and install the extensions from the aforementioned link. The following screenshot shows how the extension is installed:

When you click on the **Install Now** button, the add-on is installed. Then go to **Tools | Menu Option** and you will find **SQLite Manager**. Once you click on that option, the following screen will appear:

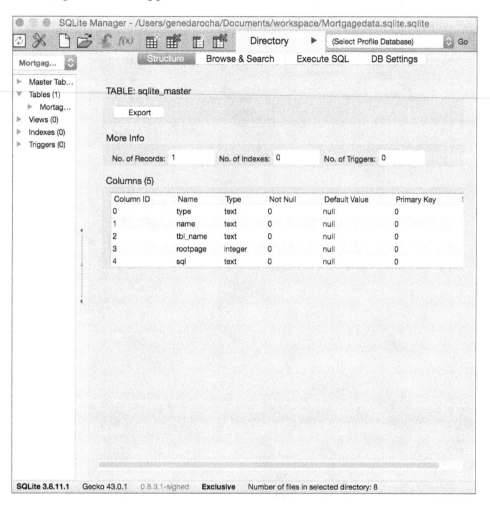

In order to add data to the system, the database must be created.

When you click on the **Install Now** button, the add-on is installed. Once you go to **Tools | Menu Option**, you will see the **SQLite Manager** option. When you click on that option, the following screen is seen.

Create the new database and ensure that a table is created for this small test application with SQLite. In this scenario, we have a database called `Mortgagedata.sqlite`, and a table called `Mortgage_data` with two fields: `mortgage_rollno` and `mortgage_name`.

The following screenshot shows the screens to call up **SQL Manager** in Firefox:

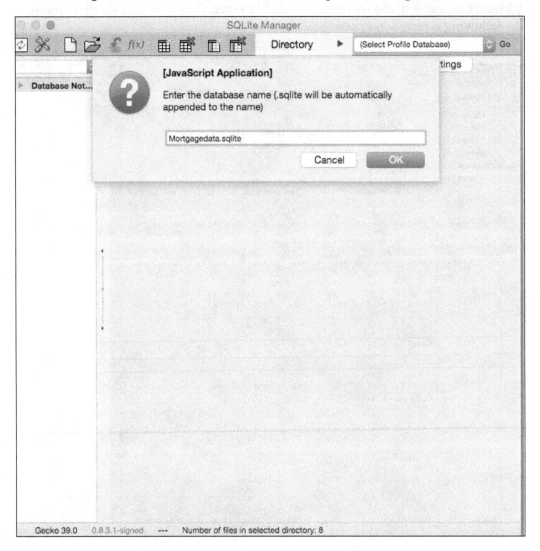

When you click on the **SQL Manager** option to create a database, a pop up will be displayed where the user enters the database name, as shown in the following screenshot:

Next, after the database is created, the user has to select a disk directory to store the database in, as shown in the next screenshot:

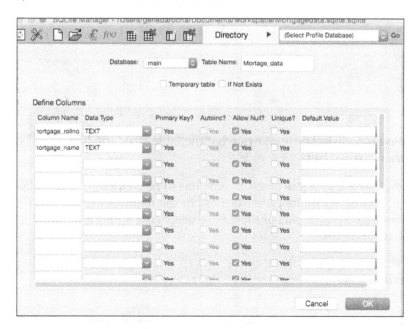

Next, you need to create a table, as shown in the preceding screenshot, with two rows:

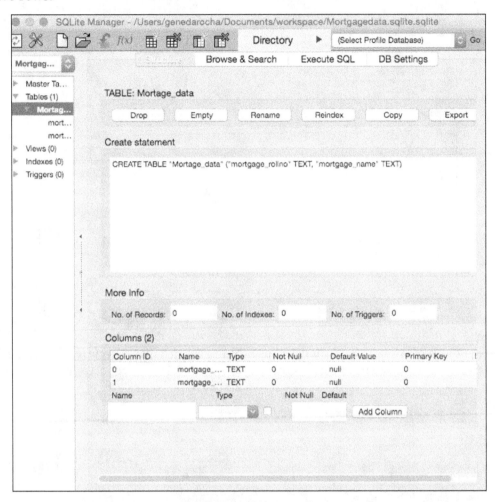

The preceding screenshot now shows what the table structure looks like before further work is carried out.

Next, a class, that is a subclass of NSObject, has to be created. Call this class Mortgage_data and set up its properties as per the requirements of this test scenario. These properties will form part of the database schema and foundations for your small database and table:

```
Class Mortgage_data: NSObject {
    Varmortgage_rollno: String = String()
    Varmortgage_name: String = String()
}
```

Using FMDB

FMDB is a SQLite library written on top of SQLite to handle database operations easier.

Since FMDB is built in Objective-C, a bridging header is required to link it up with the simple app. A .h file has to be included, which is FMDatabase.h.

This is required to ensure that the linking works for the Objective-C and Swift technology produce the results we want. Next, we need to create a database in SQLite Manager and copy it to the right place.

In the following code, we show the function to copy a database. In this instance, we need to create and use a function called copyFile, which will copy the files to the application's document directory. Methods such as applicationDidFinishLaunch work with AppDelegate by passing the database name in, as part of the requirements argument.

See the following class:

```
class func copyFile(fileName:NSString){
    var database_path:NSString=getPath(fileName)
    var MortgageManager=NSFileManager.defaultManager()
    if !MortageManager.fileExistsAtPath(database_path){
    var fromthePath:NSString= NSBundle.mainBundle().resourcePath.strin
gByAppendingPathComponent(fileName)
    MortgageManager.copyItemAtPath(fromPath,toPath:database_path,
error: nil)
    }
}
```

When using the FMDB way of interacting with SQLite, a class called ModelManager is created as part of NSObject{}, so that a variety of functions can reside, or be inserted, within it. This is mandatory and is shown in the next code snippet.

In the following code, you will see that after the database object has been copied, it needs to be initialized, a Swift file has to be named and added to the ModelManager, and a shared instance of the type of ModelManager has to be defined out of the class block, as shown in the following:

```
let mortgage_instance=ModelManager()
```

Then, set up the database object for the FMDB, namely, the FMDatabase object, and together with the database object, set up and reset it as shown in the following:

```
var database:FMDatabase?= nil
class var instance:ModelManager{
mortgage_instance.database=FMDatabase(path:Util.getPath("Mortgagedata.
sqlite"))
var Mydatapath=Util.getPath("Mortgagedata.sqlite")
println("The Current Path is> : \(Mydatapath)")
return mortgage_instance
}
```

The next part of the process is to interrogate the database with the following command, the insert command, as an example wrapped in the assigned value Mortage_Inserted. The other class, like ModelManager, will have the Mobile_data method added to it. The ModelManager method is then trying to open the Mortgage database by using the method for opening, namely, the FMDatabase class. Then the executeUpdate method is allocated and used as part of the FMDatabase class to push and pass down the SQL query and the input parameters. To finish this off, part of the operation, the close method, is used. See the following code on how the database is connected:

```
func addMortageData(Mortage_Data:Mortgage_data)-> Bool {
        mortgage_instance.database!.open()
        let Mortage_Inserted= Mortgage_instance.database!.
executeUpdate("INSERT INTO Mortgage_Data (mortgage_rollno, mortgage_
name) VALUES (?, ?)",withArgumentsInArray:[Mortgage_data.mortgage_
rollno,Mortgage_data.mortgage_name])
        mortgage_instance.database!.close()
        return isInserted
    }
```

The Insert Button has an action method; call this method to send through the Mortage_data class, which holds the mortgage_rollno and mortgage_name field names, as shown in the following:

```
@IBAction func btnInsertClicked(sender: AnyObject) {
var mortgage_data: Mortgage_data = Mortgage_data()
Mortgage_data.mortgage_rollno = tmp_ Mortgage_data.mortgage_rollno.
text
Mortgage_data.studentName = Mortgage_data.mortgage_name.text
var Mortgage_insert = ModelManager.instance.MortgageData(Mortgage)
if Mortgage_insert {
Util.invokeAlertMethod("", MortgageBody: " Data Inserted ", delegate:
nil)
        } else {
```

```
Util.invokeAlertMethod("", MortgageBody: "Error in inserting data",
delegate: nil)
            }


    Mortgage_data.tmp_rollno.text = ""
    Mortgage_data.tmp_name.text = ""
    Mortgage_data.tmp_rollno =.becomeFirstResponder()
}
```

FMDB is well documented and popular on the Internet. Next, the actual SQL query is passed through the `executeUpdate` method, which is part of the `FMDatabase` class and is linked up as parameters, as part of an argument:

```
func Mortgage_Updatedata(Mortage_data: Mortgage_Data) -> Bool {
    ModelManager.instance.database!.open()
    let Mortgage_Info_Updated {
 = sharedInstance.database!.executeUpdate("UPDATE Mortgage_data
SET Mortgage_name=? WHERE Mortgage_rollno=?",withArgumentsInArray:
[Mortgage_data.Name, Mortgage_data.rollno])
Mortgageinstance.database!.close()
return Mortgage_Info_Updated
}
```

The following code shows how the `@IBAction` function is called using the `btnUpdateClicked` function with the relevant fields and text information, to perform the update based on the click of the button called `btnUpdateClicked`:

```
@IBActionfuncMortgage_UpdateClicked(sender:AnyObject){
    var Mortgage_data:Mortgage_data=Mortgage_data()
    Mortgage_data.mortgage_rollno =tmp_mortgage_rollno.text
    Mortgage_data.mortgage_name=tmp_mortgage_name.text

    var Mortgage_Data:Mortgage_data=Mortgage_data()
    var tmp_roll_no: String ="mortgage_rollno"
    var tmp_name: String ="mortgage_name"

var Mortgage_Info_Updated = ModelManager.instance.
updateStudentData(Mortgage_data)
if Mortgage_Info_Updated {
Util.invokeAlertMethod("", strBody: "Mortgage Record has been updated
", delegate: nil)
} else {
Util.invokeAlertMethod("", strBody: "Error in updating the Mortgage
record", delegate: nil)
}
```

```
Mortgage_data.tmp_rollno.text=""
Mortgage_data.tmp_name.text=""
Mortgage_data.tmp_rollno=.becomeFirstResponder()
}
```

To perform the `delete` operation, use the `DeleteMortgateData` method. First, the `ModelManager` class is used to open the database, using the `FMDatabase` class as utilized previously. Thereafter, again use the `executeUpdate` method, and using an argument, pass the SQL `delete` query and close the database by invoking the `close` method, as defined in the `FMDatabase` class. Details of this operation are as follows:

```
func deleteStudentData(Mortgage_data:Mortgage_Data)-> Bool {
    Mortgageinstance.database!.open()
let Mortgage_isDeleted_var= Mortgageinstance.database!.
executeUpdate("DELETE FROM Mortgage_data WHERE Mortgage_data_rollno=?"
,withArgumentsInArray:[Mortgagedata.name])
sharedInstance.database!.close()
return Mortgage_isDeleted
}
```

As previously used, the same `ModelManager` method is used for SQL operations:

```
@IBAction func btnDeleteClicked(sender:AnyObject){
var Mortgage_data:Mortgage_data=Mortgage_data()
    Mortgage_data.mortgage_rollno =tmp_mortgage_rollno.text
Mortgage_data.mortgage_name=tmp_mortgage_name.text

var isDeleted_var=ModelManager.instance.deleteStudentData(studentInfo)
if isDeleted_var{
Util.invokeAlertMethod("",strBody:"Record Deleted", delegate: nil)
}else{
Util.invokeAlertMethod("",strBody:"Error- On Deleting Record",
delegate: nil)
}
    Mortgage_data.tmp_rollno.text=""
    Mortgage_data.tmp_name.text=""
    Mortgage_data.tmp_rollno=.becomeFirstResponder()
}
```

The next operation is the `SelectMortgageData` operation, which will be added to the `ModelManager` method. This will open the database by using the `open` method within the `FMDatabase` class. This is then followed by the `executeQuery` method, using the `FMDatabase` class, which accepts the input SQL query:

```
func SelectMortgageData () {
    Mortgageinstance.database!.open()
var mortgage_resultSet:FMResultSet!= Mortgageinstance.database!.
executeQuery("SELECT * FROM Mortgage_data",withArgumentsInArray: nil)
        var tmp_roll_no: String ="mortgage_rollno"
        var tmp_name: String ="mortgage_name"
if resultSet{
while mortgage_resultSet.next(){
    println("roll no data is : \(mortgage_resultSet.
stringForColumn(tmp_roll_no))")
    println("name data is : \(mortgage_resultSet.stringForColumn(tmp_
name))"
}
}Mortgageinstance.database!.close()
}
```

The following method is called from the previous action:

```
@IBAction func btnDisplayRecordClicked(sender:AnyObject){
    ModelManager.instance.MortgageData()
    }
```

The SQLite scheme using Firefox can be viewed as shown in the following screenshot. Go to Firefox, and under the **Tools** menu, invoke **SQLite Manager**. Click on the **Mortgage Manager** table and you can see the structure of the table, as shown in the following screenshot:

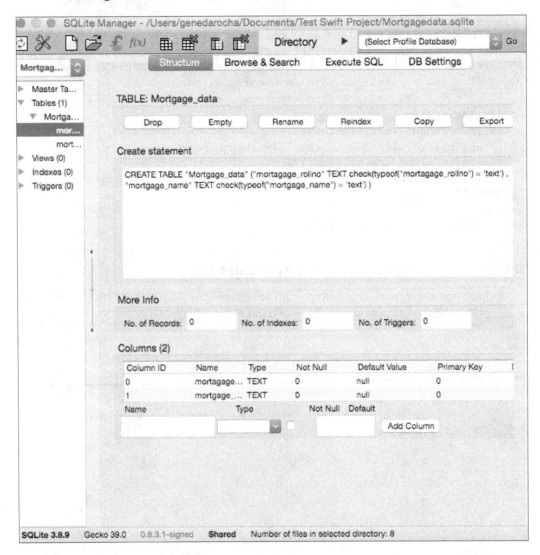

An alternate method for using FMDB this way is to use it directly in the Swift programming language, as shown in the following code. When setting up Xcode with Swift, you will be prompted for the bridging component for linking them up, but it can be done as described here.

The code is added in the place where the `IBAction` is set up. The method will require the use of the `SaveMortgageData` action method, which will open the database, take text/information from the data fields, build an SQL database, and execute the statement. Once the operation is complete, the database will be closed. Then the text fields will be initialized, ready for the next input. Therefore, the `IBAction` method using the default template will have to be modified as follows:

```
@IBAction func SaveMortgageData(sender: AnyObject) {
let Mortgage_data_save = FMDatabase(path: Database_path as String)

if Mortgage_data_save.open() {

let insertdata = "INSERT INTO Mortgage_data (mortgage_rollno,
mortgage_name) VALUES ('\(tmp_mortgage_rollno.text)', '\(tmp_mortgage_
name.text)')"

let mortgage_result = Mortgage_data_save.executeUpdate(insertdata,
            withArgumentsInArray: nil)


        if !mortgage_result {
Msg_info.text = "Error inserting Mortgage Details"
println("Error: \(Mortgage_data_save.Mortgage_ErrorMessage())")
            } else {
Msg_info.text = "Mortgage Details inserted to system"
tmp_mortgage_rollno.text = ""
tmp_mortgage_name.text = ""}
    } else {
println("Error: \(Mortgage_data_save.Mortgage_ErrorMessage())")
    }
}
```

After using this creation process and method for an application that is created with Swift and SQLite, you can see how the basic components and the `SQLite 3` library have been successfully added to the new project.

Summary

In this chapter, you had a quick look at how Xcode works with Swift. This chapter showed you some examples and ideas, and exposed the app development environment Xcode to you. We used the FMDB classes and methods to access the database and perform a variety of commands. There are some basic, but intuitive examples of how Swift works with iOS. Apple wrote this language to become the next leap in development for all developers in the next 20 years. It has also become open source as well.

In the next chapter, you will find out how Xcode can be used with PhoneGap and HTML5, and the use of SQL statements, embedded in HTML5, compiled with PhoneGap, and run as an app.

7
iOS Development with PhoneGap and HTML5

When PhoneGap was first introduced, Apple refused to accept apps created by PhoneGap as genuine, because they were not native, and were interpreted. But this has changed, partly because there are so many alternatives, partly because they were losing out on hundreds or thousands of apps to competitors, and partly because of the sheer ease of development compared to that of the past. These were the driving forces behind the change.

When code is written using PhoneGap with HTML5, you can deploy it on a certain target or platform, such as iOS or Android, or many versions are created by default, for the Apple App Store or the Android store, among others. This is the benefit of using a single code base, a newer and easier language such as HTML5, and a cross-platform development tool such as PhoneGap.

In this chapter, we will look at how to use Xcode with PhoneGap to integrate and compile with source code including HTML5. We will show you how to write code using SQLite and SQL statements and enter code directly into HTML5, which is then preprocessed by PhoneGap. We will cover all the aspects of creating a default Apple Xcode application from start to finish using the SQLite database for data storage, and using PhoneGap and HTML5 as a start.

HTML5 and PhoneGap development

Because it is easier to develop mobile and tablet apps using HTML5, PhoneGap, and generally, cross-development tools, there seems to be software snobbery, where some people think that HTML5 development is somewhat not as skilled as native development. There have been some very bad native developments built so far, but the same could apply to HTML5 or other mobile apps on the app stores.

Using these modern cross-development tools is a good and quick way if you want to build prototypes from designs that give and show the look and feel, and show some functionality too. Cross-browser technology will not perform as quickly or efficiently as a native app and, as mentioned, it has a reputation for not being as real as native apps. With the growth of mobile technology, there has been a high growth of HTML5 apps available, because they are much faster to design, develop, and produce, compared to native apps.

There are pitfalls for those web developers who think that they can just put an app together for mobiles to produce something comparable to a desktop. Well, they are wrong. Anyone who builds a mobile app for iOS, for example, must read their human guidelines document, which will outline how to actually take into consideration the user experience, the way to design buttons and journeys, and how best to build something that fits in the iOS ecosystem. Google/Android has fewer checks, but as their app store grows, I am sure there will be more or different types of controls enforced.

Web developers must understand the limitations of their destination devices for these apps. Mobiles, including smartphones, actually don't have the processing power of a desktop, and web developers must be aware of how programming principles can be applied within these types of developments.

It is great to try new software technology; if you have an idea, then try to create, test it, and submit your app to the App Store. But if you take some person and get them to try to create a native app, they have to learn a whole new language and way of doing things. It's going to take a lot longer until they are even able to produce a working mobile app, but by that time they will have quite a bit of experience. There are applications that have a mixed mode of native code, combined with cross-development code such as HTML5. In practice, although these work, there are huge pitfalls in performance and they are limited as well.

There are advantages to building and using native apps and applications for specific mobile devices or operating systems, which are usually installed on your phone via an app store. These benefits include speed of development, the same app across the product range, one set of code, and a change queue for the app. Native is the best way to code ideally, but if you have web skills and you don't want to learn a new programming language, and you want to create an HTML5 app, using PhoneGap delivered on iOS, Android, or Windows may be an alternate way of using your skills.

With advances in HTML5 and PhoneGap API options, there are many new functions, including those of camera manipulation, for example, which can be done via some basic commands. With a good designer, a decent app using HTML5 can be made quite quickly and economically.

Mobile developers need to be educated on performance deliverables to build apps, which are skills they can use again and again. The benefits will be used on all the apps they produce.

The advantages of a mobile app surpass the straightforward usage of a mobile website. Some advantages are listed here:

- A variety of programming languages such as Swift, Objective-C (iOS), Java (Android), or C# (Windows Phone) can be used to deliver the end app, for example

- All the "controls" and the API are native in design and development, and are interrogated and approved by the app stores from Apple, Google, or Windows

- The other benefit of using native is that there is no reliance on any outside technology for it to work, and there is the possibility of working offline if required

The mobile web application by definition would have less access to the low-level functionalities of a device and system calls. Due to enhanced development of the APIs and higher-level languages such as HTML5, CSS, or JavaScript, this is changing through software updates and upgrades. By using the mobile web/app solutions for mobile sites, app store approval is not required, and by ensuring proper code design, the same application can work with a variety of devices and device sizes, and different mobile or desktop operating systems or browsers. Information is served to the app, and there are no offline facilities, unlike native.

HTML5 is praised as easy, unlike the native facilities offered by native code.

An HTML5 framework

Functionality, like memory allocation and usage, animations, and a variety of other options, will define what a good HTML5 framework is. This framework does offer good access to mobile phone devices, such as the camera, or some other internal information that only a native app could previously access. These factors go far in deciding the type of framework to use.

Just because some frameworks or JavaScript libraries are popular in one area does not necessarily mean they are not required in another. For example, the jQuery JavaScript framework is very popular due to many programmers having used it in the past for large or small projects.

It will be difficult for an end user to distinguish native and HTML5 development when the app is running. However, the way it is installed will determine whether it is a web or native app. Not that it matters to the end user, but users expect a great look and feel, richness in technology, easy and quick navigation, and that the app actually solves their issue, which is the functionality of the application in the first place.

Hybrid applications

There are some misconceptions about the use of hybrid HTML5 apps. Users think that hybrid applications cannot store offline data in a database such as SQLite. Hybrid apps can work online and offline. They do not need to be connected all the time for it to work. PhoneGap with HTML5 gives more facilities, functionalities, and options.

The standard storage mechanism for HTML5 apps is the local storage on the device itself, that is, the database used is SQLite. If you are not connected online, data can be stored locally. Once the database is connected, it will upload data from the local database.

A common thought is that HTML5 is out of its league when it comes to native. However, today, in-app purchases, Game Centre, executing background tasks, accessing the GPS and the camera, and even Bluetooth, can be accessed via HTML5. PhoneGap is used where a native wrapper is required for an HTML5 app. There are some differences in the way native and hybrid/cross-development apps work, like PhoneGap compared to Objective-C. Hybrid/HTML5 apps are slower, and although the functionality of HTML5 has increased, it does not match native yet.

An Xcode project with PhoneGap, HTML5, and Swift

Before we start to do anything, you have to start by building the environment and the software tools, and making some minor configurations to get everything ready. The app itself will be simple, and outline the process of creating an app for PhoneGap and HTML5.

You need to download the Xcode software to get the project working.

For Apple users, the Xcode command-line tool, and the Apache Cordova product can be downloaded from: `https://itunes.apple.com/us/app/xcode/id497799835?mt=12`.

To get the command-lines tools for Xcode and other components, download them from `https://developer.apple.com/downloads/index.action`. You need to be a registered as an Apple developer to be able to download any extra components. A second and easier method for PhoneGap is to just download the software from the site and install it, as opposed to using the older, command-line way.

The following screenshot shows you Xcode in the iTunes Store:

The next screenshot shows the software available for a developer when you log in through an Apple Developer account. Only the command-line Xcode tools are required. It also shows you the command-line tools that can be downloaded and installed:

The next part of the process is to download the Cordova module of the software, as shown in the software in the following screenshot. This is the location of the latest Apache/Cordova release. PhoneGap was acquired by Adobe in 2011, and the project itself was donated to the **Apache Software Foundation** (**ASF**). There are two ways of using PhoneGap. One is its cloud-based service to build apps and the second is the local/manual version to build and package apps the PhoneGap CLI way. We will be using the PhoneGap CLI way in our first setup, as follows:

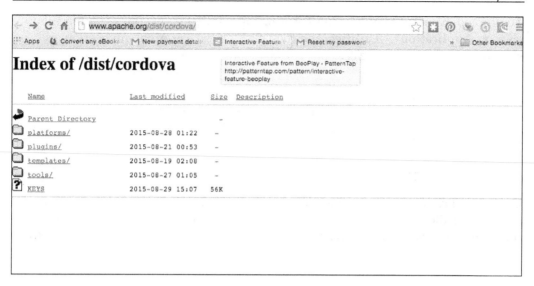

Download the Cordova software to the Downloads folder, unpack it, and within the cordova-ios directory, you'll find all the necessary components to use PhoneGap/Cordova with Xcode to create a simple app. The following screenshot shows the directory structure for the Cordova/PhoneGap system. As you can see, PhoneGap supports a variety of technologies and cross-platforms:

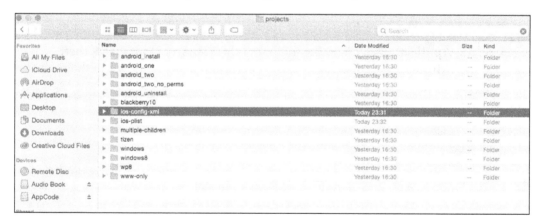

To proceed, we need to invoke the **Terminal** app. Initially, on your OS X machine, click on **Applications | Utilities**, and then click on the **Terminal** application, as shown in the following image:

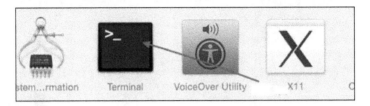

Once you click on the image, the following window for the **Terminal** app can be seen. It will allow you to carry on with the process of setting up the environment and required components. This is where you can carry out the necessary commands to install it:

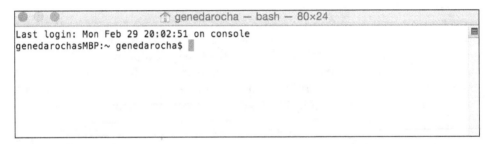

Click on the **Applications** icon on the toolbar at the bottom of the screen, then click on the **Utilities** folder, then click on the **Terminal** icon, as shown in the following screenshot:

After selecting the **Applications** icon, click on the **Utilities** folder:

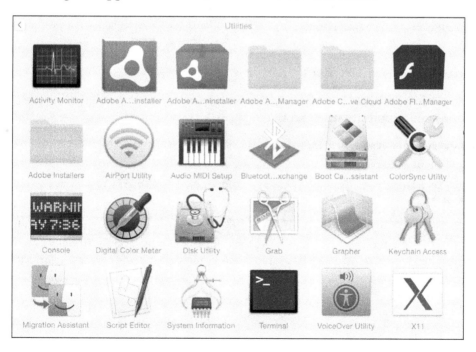

Once the **Terminal** window is clicked, the following window is displayed:

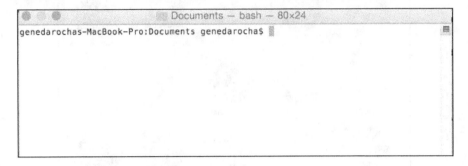

Once you're in this directory, perform the following commands: the first one is to create a project, and the second one is to create a directory with your app name:

```
$cd ~/Documents
$cordova create hello com.example.helloHelloWorld
```

A package for the Hello program has now been created using Cordova. Before you start to build any projects, the system needs to know which platforms to target, for example, Android, iOS, or Windows. Cordova now has the iOS platform added to it, as shown in the following code:

```
$ cd hello
$ cordova platform add ios
```

Once a platform is added, performing the following command will outline the platforms your application can work on:

```
$ cordova platforms ls
Installed platforms: ios 3.7.0
Available platforms: amazon-fireos, android, blackberry10, browser,
firefoxos
```

Within the Hello application, perform a directory listing with ls-1 and you will see a variety of directories, such as platforms. Set the platforms directory as the default. Then perform an ls-1 listing to see a variety of directories, including the HelloWorld.xcodeproj file.

Once you open the `Hello.xcodeproj` file, Xcode will wake up and you will see the project name. You can enter a company identifier as well. See the following screenshot.

You will be prompted for a simulator phone to be selected upon execution. Select **iOS simulator for iPhone 6.0**. Next, select the simulator and click on the **Run** button to compile, link, build, and execute the simple application. You will be presented with the Cordova image, as shown in the following screenshot, and the `Hello` app will then be displayed:

At this stage, you have set up an Xcode project with Cordova or PhoneGap and some basic code. Now it is time to add some HTML5 code into the mix to show how both aspects of PhoneGap/iOS and SQLite work together.

In addition to the method used previously to install Cordova, the easiest way is to download and install PhoneGap directly, without going through the command-line method. Click on the **Download** button on the PhoneGap download page at `http://phonegap.com/download`.

The process may alter for some of its versions, but will usually be the same for most of them. Next, the .zip file is downloaded, so open it up and extract the files to a directory. Then install the PhoneGap program, which will deliver the interface, and once this step is complete, create an Xcode project, as shown in the following screenshot. Since you have done this before, doing it this way is even easier:

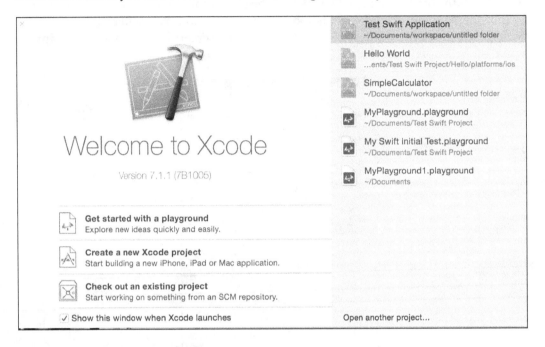

When you've performed the preceding task, like with previous installations, an extra icon for PhoneGap will appear. Since you have installed the components required for Xcode and PhoneGap to work together, you are now ready to start developing.

The following screenshot shows how to select the PhoneGap app type:

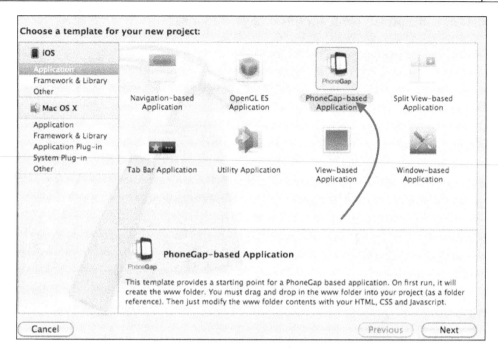

When creating a Cordova application, you must select the Cordova-based application template, as shown in the following screenshot:

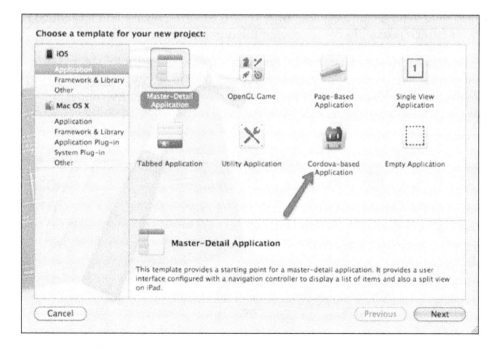

Next, choose the project name for this project—enter `Hello`:

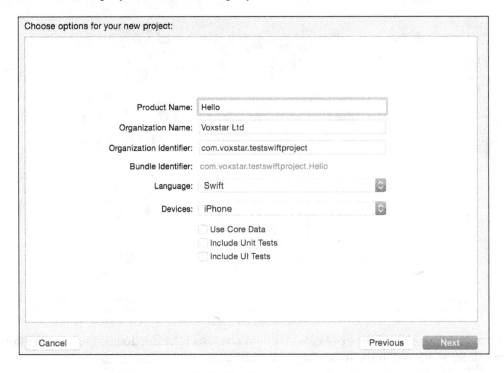

The next field is for a company identifier ID. Like before, please add a unique identifier, which is usually the reverse of the domain name.

This is a standard way to install the PhoneGap framework with Xcode. In your browser, go to `https://nodejs.org/` and press the **Install** button to download the JavaScript library called `node.js`. Finally, enter the admin/username and password details to install the software locally:

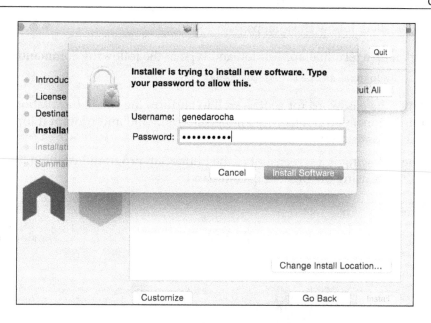

Your successful installation message will be as follows:

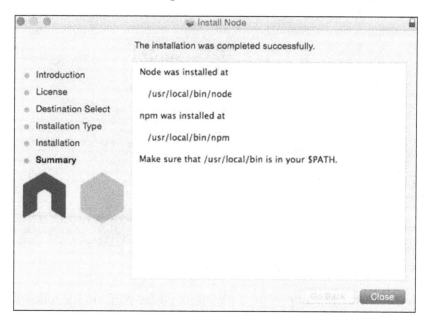

Once it is installed, follow these steps:

1. Open up a terminal application and type in the following command:

   ```
   $    sudo npm install -g phonegap
   ```

2. Enter the password for root as well to perform the actual installation. Once this is done, you can use the PhoneGap command and prompt it for some help or assistance.

3. The following is a screenshot of the PhoneGap program installing the software using the preceding command:

```
genedarochas-MacBook-Pro:tmp genedarocha$ sudo npm install -g phonegap


> ws@0.4.31 install /usr/local/lib/node_modules/phonegap/node_modules/connect-ph
onegap/node_modules/socket.io/node_modules/engine.io/node_modules/ws
> (node-gyp rebuild 2> builderror.log) || (exit 0)

  CXX(target) Release/obj.target/bufferutil/src/bufferutil.o
    WARN engine xmlbuilder@2.2.1: wanted: {"node":"0.8.x || 0.10.x"} (current: {
"node":"0.12.7","npm":"2.11.3"})

> ws@0.4.31 install /usr/local/lib/node_modules/phonegap/node_modules/connect-ph
onegap/node_modules/socket.io/node_modules/socket.io-client/node_modules/engine.
io-client/node_modules/ws
> (node-gyp rebuild 2> builderror.log) || (exit 0)

  CXX(target) Release/obj.target/bufferutil/src/bufferutil.o
/usr/local/bin/phonegap -> /usr/local/lib/node_modules/phonegap/bin/phonegap.js
phonegap@5.2.2 /usr/local/lib/node_modules/phonegap
├── pluralize@0.0.4
├── colors@0.6.0-1
├── semver@1.1.0
├── minimist@0.1.0
├── qrcode-terminal@0.9.4
├── shelljs@0.1.4
├── phonegap-build@0.9.2 (colors@0.6.2, qrcode-terminal@0.8.0, optimist@0.3.7, s
helljs@0.0.9, phonegap-build-api@0.3.3)
├── prompt@0.2.11 (revalidator@0.1.8, pkginfo@0.3.0, read@1.0.7, utile@0.2.1, wi
nston@0.6.2)
├── cordova@5.2.0 (underscore@1.7.0, q@1.0.1, nopt@3.0.1, cordova-lib@5.2.0)
├── connect-phonegap@0.17.0 (home-dir@0.1.2, connect-inject@0.3.2, ip@0.3.1, req
uest-progress@0.3.1, walkdir@0.0.8, adm-zip@0.4.7, shelljs@0.2.6, http-proxy@1.8
.1, node-static@0.7.0, gaze@0.4.3, tar@0.1.19, localtunnel@1.3.0, useragent@2.0.
3, archiver@0.14.3, request@2.33.0, connect@2.12.0, socket.io@1.0.4)
genedarochas-MacBook-Pro:tmp genedarocha$
genedarochas-MacBook-Pro:tmp genedarocha$
```

4. Next, to actually set up your application, please perform the following commands. First position and set the default to the right directory within the terminal application program.

5. Run the `$ phonegap create Hello` command. (`Hello` is your app's name.) Next, set the default to the application directory in which you just created your PhoneGap app.

The following screenshot shows the local directory and the creation of a new Cordova project called `Hello`. A new project has been created with all the necessary components for this new test app:

```
genedarochasMBP:~ genedarocha$ pwd
/Users/genedarocha
genedarochasMBP:~ genedarocha$ cd Documents
genedarochasMBP:Documents genedarocha$ cd Test(
-bash: syntax error near unexpected token `('
genedarochasMBP:Documents genedarocha$ cd Test*
genedarochasMBP:Test Swift Project genedarocha$ pwd
/Users/genedarocha/Documents/Test Swift Project
genedarochasMBP:Test Swift Project genedarocha$
genedarochasMBP:Test Swift Project genedarocha$ phonegap create HelloWorld
Creating a new cordova project.

genedarochasMBP:Test Swift Project genedarocha$ 
```

Next, at the prompt, perform the following command to run the application in iOS. Run the $ `phonegap run ios` command. If you run the iOS project from anywhere, the following error will be displayed. But if you set the default to the right directory (`Hello`), then it will work:

```
/Users/genedarocha/Documents/Test Swift Project
genedarochasMBP:Test Swift Project genedarocha$ ls -l
total 152
drwxr-xr-x  8 genedarocha  staff    272  3 Sep 17:54 Hello
drwxr-xr-x  7 genedarocha  staff    238  1 Mar 23:28 HelloWorld
-rw-r--r--@ 1 genedarocha  staff  65536 16 Aug  2015 Mortgagedata.sqlite
drwxr-xr-x  7 genedarocha  staff    238  1 Oct 11:17 My Swift initial Test.p
round
drwxr-xr-x  7 genedarocha  staff    238 30 Sep 00:26 MyPlayground.playground
drwxr-xr-x  5 genedarocha  staff    170 21 Aug  2015 New Swift Test
drwxr-xr-x  7 genedarocha  staff    238 12 Aug  2015 Test Swift Project
drwxr-xr-x  5 genedarocha  staff    170 12 Aug  2015 Test Swift Project.xcod

drwxr-xr-x  4 genedarocha  staff    136 12 Aug  2015 Test Swift ProjectTests
-rw-r--r--  1 root         staff   9186  1 Sep  2015 npm-debug.log
genedarochasMBP:Test Swift Project genedarocha$ cd HelloWorld
genedarochasMBP:HelloWorld genedarocha$ ls
config.xml      hooks          platforms          plugins          www
genedarochasMBP:HelloWorld genedarocha$ phonegap run ios
[phonegap] executing 'cordova platform add --save ios'...
[phonegap] completed 'cordova platform add --save ios'
[phonegap] executing 'cordova run ios'...
```

1. In the next code, you can see the call to PhoneGap to get the app working. The process has been made much smoother, to operate and work for the benefit of creating apps.

2. Next, we will add some HTML5 to the source code:

```
genedarochasMBP:HelloWorld genedarocha$ ls
config.xml      hooks           platforms       plugins         www
genedarochasMBP:HelloWorld genedarocha$ phonegap run ios
[phonegap] executing 'cordova platform add --save ios'...
[phonegap] completed 'cordova platform add --save ios'
[phonegap] executing 'cordova run ios'...
[phonegap] completed 'cordova run ios'
genedarochasMBP:HelloWorld genedarocha$
```

3. Once the new Hello basic application has been compiled and built, the following image will appear, showing the Cordova system. This is very important, and it is key to know that PhoneGap and its Cordova components are registered and working as intended:

4. We can now develop this app further by adding some SQLite and HTML5 code. It is very important to get the base of the product set up, tested, and ready for further development:

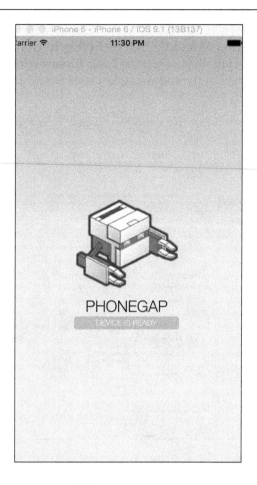

 Further information about PhoneGap can be found
at docs.phonegap.com.

To open the code base using the Xcode project file (Hello World.xcodeproj),
follow these steps:

1. Click on the file in the **Hello Directory | Platforms | iOS**, which will then
   bring up the Xcode, code, and source files.

2. The following is a screenshot of the Xcode source file area for our test application. In order to add the SQLite library to your project, click on the **Build Phases** tab, then select the **Link Binary with Libraries** menu option and add one of the following libraries from `libsqlite3.dylib` or `libsqlite3.0.dylib`:

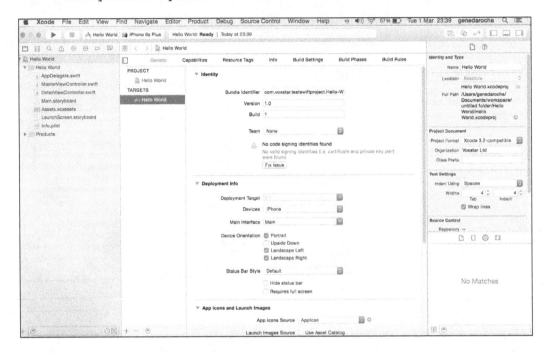

Next, open the `Hello` Xcode project file as shown in the following screenshot. Within the structure, expand the Xcode project to reveal the HTML file within. Then add some of the following HTML5 code into the `.html` file, and compile, and run it:

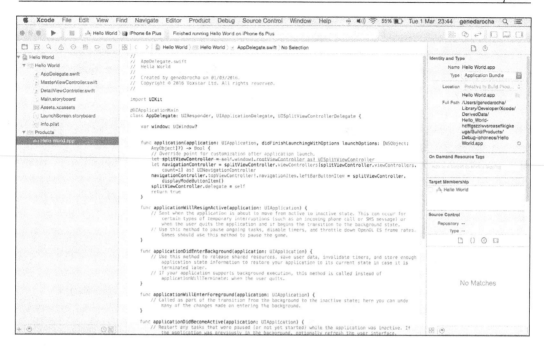

Add the following HTML5 code, which will perform some simple SQLite statements. It will take a couple of input numbers; check for the existence of a local database/local tables, create necessary tables, store the data, and retrieve it. This code will be part of Xcode; use Cordova/PhoneGap to compile the source code, and execute the results to run the mobile app. Once you enter the code into the `index.html` file within the `Hello` app, save the file, and quit Xcode.

This is a simple HTML5 app, which creates a database called `testdb`. It checks to see whether the `BLOGS` table is created. If not, then it will create the `BLOGS` table, enter two records for blog information, and display the data on the screen. You can see the following code and results:

```
<!DOCTYPE HTML>
<html>

<head>

<script type="text/javascript">

var db = openDatabase('testdb', '1.0', 'Test DB', 2 * 1024 *
1024);
```

```
var msg;

                db.transaction(function (tx) {
tx.executeSql('CREATE TABLE IF NOT EXISTS BLOGS (id unique,
log)');
tx.executeSql('INSERT INTO BLOGS (id, log) VALUES (1, "This is
test blog 1")');
tx.executeSql('INSERT INTO BLOGS (id, log) VALUES (2, "This is
test blog 2")');
                        msg = '<p>Blog message created and row
inserted.</p>';
document.querySelector('#status').innerHTML =  msg;
                        });


                        db.transaction(function (tx) {
tx.executeSql('SELECT * FROM BLOGS', [], function (tx, results) {
var len = results.rows.length, i;

                                        msg =
"<p>Found rows: " + len + "</p>";
document.querySelector('#status').innerHTML +=  msg;

for (i = 0; i < len; i++){
                                        msg =
"<p><b>" + results.rows.item(i).log + "</b></p>";
document.querySelector('#status').innerHTML +=  msg;
                                        }
                                        }, null);
                        });


</script>

</head>

<body>
<div id="status" name="status">Status Message</div>
</body>

</html>
```

1. Click on the **Terminal** app, and within the **Terminal** app, set the default to the `Hello` app directory, as shown in the following code:

```
-bash: jpwd: command not found
genedarochasMBP:HelloWorld genedarocha$ pwd
/Users/genedarocha/Documents/Test Swift Project/HelloWorld
genedarochasMBP:HelloWorld genedarocha$
genedarochasMBP:HelloWorld genedarocha$
genedarochasMBP:HelloWorld genedarocha$ pwd
/Users/genedarocha/Documents/Test Swift Project/HelloWorld
genedarochasMBP:HelloWorld genedarocha$
```

2. Perform the `phonegap run ios` command, which will bring up the PhoneGap/Cordova start screen, as shown in the following screenshot. This shows that the Cordova/PhoneGap environment has been set up properly, and the application will start to execute:

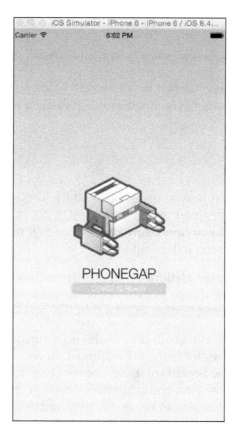

3. The following is the output from the `Hello` app. It shows two records, which are inserted, and then displayed. It is a simple process, but the workflow is the same as we discussed:

After this exercise, you have learned how to install Node.js and Cordova, and how to create a simple iOS application, run Xcode, and simulate a simple application using an iPhone 6.

Summary

In this chapter, you learned how to use Xcode and PhoneGap with SQLite and HTML5. Hopefully, it has helped you to perform iOS development with these technologies, and showed you how using PhoneGap/SQLite can enhance how quickly apps can be delivered to the end user.

It is also a cross-development platform, where the source is created once and delivered to a variety of platforms in a quick-format generation method. HTML5 works with Xcode, Swift, and PhoneGap in a cohesive and quick way.

In the next chapter, we will talk about future advances, further features, and SQLite functionality. This will be useful in the development process, to get better and more controlled applications. The benefits of using one codebase for multiple platforms is very beneficial to both developers and customers. The next chapter will also be an aid and guide on how these features can be used in new and updated apps in the future.

8
More Features and Advances in SQLite

This chapter will explore some new features in SQLite, and it will also cover the recent advances made in this database. This chapter will show you how SQLite is exposed to other languages and frameworks and discuss the extensions of the C API, the usage of **PhoneGap**, and other cross-platform development environments. This chapter will also outline SQLite's other features and how SQLite has advanced to ensure that all those who use it can master it quickly.

You will also look at how SQLite has changed in recent years, how it has advanced to be integrated with a variety of existing technologies, and how its simple, easy-to-use formula has guaranteed its popularity to others. The amount of apps that use database technology, without disclosing the backend or local database, is incredible. SQLite, as will be shown later, has advanced to new levels and kept its simplicity but with developers pushing it to achieve new heights and popularity.

Firefox and SQLite extensions to their browsers are available for administration purposes. SQLite has gone through several code changes, and in the future, it will continue to do so or be overtaken by something newer.

Adobe's Enterprise Management system works with PhoneGap, which uses SQLite. Because of its simple setup, there are several cases of SQLite using different technologies and integrating well.

The growth of relational database management systems to this date have been very strong, and if the data requires industrial strength, storage, and application, SQLite is the right format. However, in more recent years, solutions such as NOSQL, which purely rely on the data selected from technologies such as REST APIs or web services, have not used **RDBMS (relational database management system)** to store their data. It will be retrieved and held in a file type structure, in effect, as its own version of RDMS. SQLite does not have the industrial support of tools like **database backup** or **database recovery**. In a world of mobile devices where the growth has been intensive and beating all types of expectation, SQLite is by far the easiest and quickest one to use with a minimum time spent learning.

The **Firefox SQLite Manager** facility is a good software extension to the browser. Once installed, it can serve as an aid to various processes of the database administrator.

Its simplicity and flexibility make it great for developing and testing. There is no mechanism to ensure performance, and it is possible to tune up the library. SQLite is great for embedded applications that are somewhat fixed, single user, mobile users, and gaming information storage.

It is easy to download and install SQLite. Once this is done, it gets fired up to work.

PhoneGap plugins

Before starting to develop a software for PhoneGap with SQLite, the environment must be set up properly for the PhoneGap framework to work correctly with SQLite. The PhoneGap environment will enable the SQLite database to be set up and connected with Xcode, toward the end, to produce an iOS application.

There is also a native SQLite plugin for PhoneGap, called **Brodysoft** (refer to `https://build.phonegap.com/plugins/2368`), that provides an interface for the storage and usage of the standard Web SQL database standards.

As the demand for mobile technology, mobile apps, and mobile development grows, the need for further advancement, with products such as PhoneGap, will be demanding the following, for example:

- PhoneGap will have increased application size limits
- It will have support for different plugins, including the Cordova plugins repository `plugins.cordova.io`
- Additional PhoneGap plugins may not have to go through an approval process and can be approved easily

- There will be a facility to upload your own plugins to your own development area so that you can test them privately

To support additional plugins, which are more than 600 on the PhoneGap environment, the `source` attribute can be used.

PhoneGap plugins, unlike before, can contain compiled components such as frameworks, `.jar` files, and other related binaries. There is a lot of documentation about this procedure on the PhoneGap site. PhoneGap is now moving ahead with an `Amazon Mobile Ad Network` plugin, which will allow developers to monetize their app. This is because the `Amazon Ads` API has been created to be used within applications to facilitate advertising, and is a platform for this sole purpose. It will be used across different tablets, mobile devices, different utilities, and game apps.

The `cordova.xml` file used by **Cordova** or PhoneGap is the main parameter file where configuration changes are made to the environment.

For example, using the native Cordova/PhoneGap plugin for Android and iOS, the HTML5 Web SQL API can be used to code directly, as shown in the following. Here, the code is waiting to see if the API has been loaded before attempting to open the database:

```
<gap:plugin name="com.phonegap.plugins.example" version="0.3.3"
source="plugins.cordova.io" />

// Wait for Cordova html5 plugin to load document.
addEventListener("deviceready", onDeviceReady, false); var db;
function onDeviceReady() {    db1 =
  window.sqlitePlugin.openDatabase({name: "DB"}); }
```

 There is a plugin available and developed for the PhoneGap system `https://github.com/litehelpers/Cordova-sqlite-storage`. In order to use this plugin, add the following code to your `config.xml` file:

```
<gap:plugin name="com.millerjames01.sqlite-plugin" version="1.0.1"/>
```

This plugin is compatible with both iOS and Android operating systems and also works with Cordova.

The following piece of code is essential to ensure that a check is done, to see if the device is ready and if Cordova is ready to load:

```
// Wait for Cordova to load document.addEventListener("deviceready",
onDeviceReady, false);
```

```
// Cordova is ready function onDeviceReady()
{    var db = window.sqlitePlugin.openDatabase({name: "DB"
}


);   // ... }
```

Using the preceding plugin, it makes the inclusion of SQL directly into HTML5 easier and faster, as shown in the following:

```
Db.transaction(function(Tx1) {
   Tx1.executeSql("Create table if not exists" + " test(id integer
primary key asc, newcolumn text, []);
});
}
```

It becomes easy to add the necessary HTML content, and this works with both iOS and Android. The relationship between HTML5, SQLite, and PhoneGap to compile is an advancement of technology.

Not all the aspects of the ALTER TABLE statement are implemented in SQLite, and there is no support for the GRANT or REVOKE statements.

Extensions to the C API

SQLite binding functionality extends the popularity and diversity of the SQLite language, but it is not supported by the core developers of the database. Instead, the SQLite community takes care of these integrations, and is well-documented online. Scripting languages, such as Perl, PHP, and Python or Java, work nicely with SQLite.

The C API interface specification for SQLite has several interface elements and can be grouped into the following categories:

- Category one has a list of objects and datatypes utilized by the SQLite library. There are over a dozen objects and datatypes in it. The most meaningful and common ones are the database object called sqlite3 and the prepare statement called sqlite3_stmt.

- Category two will have its list of constants used by SQLite and are referenced by the usage of the #defines syntax in the sqlite3.h header file. These are standard constants, such as SQLITE_OPEN_READONLY.

- Category three is a list of all the functions available and the methods they use within the objects, for returning values and usage of standard constants.

For example, the int sqlite3_sleep(int); function is based on the number of milliseconds that it will suspend the execution of an instruction.

As mobiles become more powerful, there will always be an alteration to the amount of memory resources that SQLite can handle or use. The technology that is used within SQLite is called page cache. Now, page caching is important since this is how memory is used and set up for the SQLite performance. It has one I/O algorithm and two search algorithms. There is a binary search that uses the index of the table and full on brutal attack to read the full table. Since the limited decisions were made about how to write and implement them, and since it is more general and not designed for any specific application, the performance generally may not be equal to what is expected.

Although, SQLite does have an optimizer, it is not the most advanced of its type, but it is practical. In the following example, we see the creation of two tables and a join. We will use the EXPLAIN statement and then ask SQLite to see how it would get the results. As the results will begin to show, it will use one of the category formats discussed earlier in this section, which is just a major scan. It will only work properly if there is a SELECT statement with JOIN but with an index or a key on a simple query. On a complex query, you need to use the EXPLAIN statement. We just select one column from the first table and a scan of the whole table takes place:

```
sqlite> CREATE TABLE one (y, z);
sqlite> CREATE TABLE two (a, b);
sqlite> EXPLAIN QUERY PLAN SELECT A FROM one JOIN two ON one.z = two.b
WHERE y = 30;

0|0|TABLE one
1|1|TABLE two
```

In terms of page cache, SQLite, as mentioned earlier, uses a disk with a page-based format. The cache along with SQLite is pulled from disk. There is no automatic recycling of pages; it can be reused once the page is empty. Also, if a page is reused again and again, it will become fragmented, and its data will be spread across the database file, which will decrease in terms of the performance.

As mentioned previously in this book, there is **Core Data** from Apple, standard for iOS, but SQLite, which is free, is the dominant and cross-platform database solution for mobile.

With the advancement of new frameworks, there is a new technology, which aims to replace both: SQLite and Core Data. It is called **Realm**. It is free for both iOS and Android and would be a good product to investigate. While the others maybe limited, this product must ensure that it is easy to set up, use, and administer. So far, it is being used by a variety of large e-commerce and data sites, such as Pinterest or BBC. Realm.io is the location for this database software, is modern API for today's changeable market.

With Realm, there is a plugin for **Xcode**, which seems to hook in and work well as per the demo. There is a complete API reference, which works with Objective-C, Swift, and Java. Realm also has its own Realm Browser from the Apple app store, which is used as an app to manage the databases, such as the Firefox plugin for SQLite.

Write Ahead Logging with SQLite

Write Ahead Logging with SQLite, also known as **WAL**, is the standard method that states how SQLite implements the `rollback` and `commit` processes with this mobile database system. The disk access and input and output operations are more sequential, using the `WAL` methods. Using `WAL` will involve less of the `fsync()` functions and operations. It means it is more likely to work properly on different operating systems and smartphones. `WAL` is faster on most operations and provides better concurrencies, as there are no conflicts with processes reading and writing at the same time with a big reduction in any data block.

As much as there are advantages, there are also limitations to this method. `WAL` does not work efficiently with very large transactions, but much better with smaller transactions. For transactions of around 100 megabytes, it will work fine, but over a gigabyte, it will start to reduce its efficiency. There is also another issue: `WAL` could fail operations if it encounters a *disk full* error, although, an extra operation is **checkpointing**, which is embedded as a part of the system. Developers need to be aware of this checkpointing.

`WAL` and `rollback` may be slower than the current/traditional method of operation. This is because of the amount of reads and low attempts of writes on the database. This is only in the range of 1-2%. Another disadvantage is that the database page size cannot be changed when using the WAL mode even if it is an empty database. To resolve the problem, you have to restore from a backup using the provided **BACKUP API**, and you must be in a rollback journal mode in order to succeed. There is also a problem reading the **read-only WAL** databases.

WAL works by creating and writing up a copy of the original database with no changes into a new/separate rollback journal file. Changes are then directly made to the database file. If there is a crash and the system has to perform the `rollback` operation, then the unchanged original version is played back to the database file, which will change to its original state. The `commit` operation is done when the rollback journal is deleted. It is quite an effective procedure. Transactions writing to disk are always fast because the content is written only once.

The B-tree usage with SQLite

The arbitrary storage of leaf nodes and its location on the actual disk will not link up or respond to the index order or any logical positioning. Therefore, a database search algorithm is used with the right structure, to change the position and quickly output a balanced search tree or, in short, a B-tree. Each branch of data will have its leaf nodes that link or refer to the memory location that is used to store each and every table of the database.

B-tree allows sequential access, deletions, and insertions, based on the general binary search tree in a node that can have two or more children. When data is removed or added, the number of child nodes will change, and in order to maintain a specific range, some internal nodes may join or split. Every internal node within a B-tree structure will have a number of keys. Each of these keys will have a value and will be divided into subtrees. B-tree is a good way to search for data with a key associated to find the right data, but it is inefficient at search data with a query string; it uses an index to speed up this searching. B-trees are an efficient way of searching data with a key, and when executed correctly, they become very quick. This is an explanation about B-tree and how it is applied with SQLite.

Creating a simple Swift

With the advent of Swift and Swift2, there is the use of an environment called a **playground** now. It is a place where you can set up a quick environment with some code and then see the results. It is a quick, new way to use the new setup. When you start, it will have a main window and the results on the second, split one.

In Xcode, navigate to **New | Playground** and the following screenshot will be shown. Give a name to your playground. You can have several running of them under different platforms, so a meaningful name would be useful:

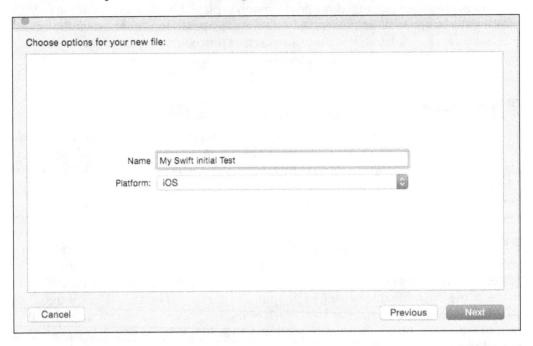

Once this is created and the **Next** button is clicked on, the following screen will appear. Here, you can create the code, test ideas and code snippets, and just try it out. It is a great and simple idea, which will help motivate existing developers, and create new developers for the future:

As you can see from the preceding screenshot, there is a split page on the right-hand side, which can be adjusted as per requirement. The code appears on the left-hand side, and the results appear on the right-hand side. In the preceding code, a call to UIKIT is made; the next line creates a variable called str and has a default string value of Hello playground.

UIKit is the core foundation of iOS framework that is used for on app development. After var is defined as str to equal Hello Playground in order to change, it should be defined as str = New Playground, which will reassign the variable to a new value. Creating a default system, using the var statement, and then assigning it, shows that the default variable value can be changed. However, if you use the let statement to say let str =new play and straight after that add str =newnewplay line, the system would throw an error, because you cannot change the value of a constant with the let command.

The playground can accept different types of data types, as you would imagine, making it a fun but productive way to get into development or test new ideas. In the next simple example, a variable called age, with a datatype of int, is set up.

A default value of 25 is given to this value. Then, take the value of age and multiply it by 10, and you will get a new value of 250, as shown in the following screenshot. This is the beauty of the playground:

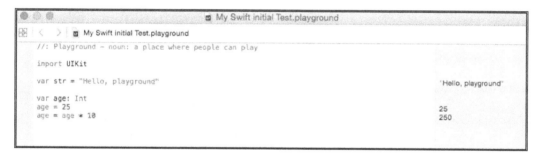

Swift has a good range of comparison operators, just as most languages, but you can use the = and > ways or the < way as well, as shown the following screenshot:

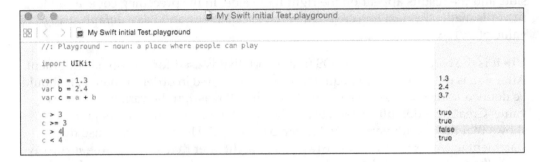

The Swift interpolation is also easier with Swift. By creating a variable and then using the command to print the name , for example, by using the \ (name) where name is variable name, as shown in the following screenshot. It is easy, but it is good to practice this again and again so that the information is locked inside your mind:

As shown in the following screenshot, the usage of the + concatenation does not work in Swift, especially the merging of string, doubles, or integers. But the expression in the next image clearly shows how \ between the name, age, or latitude can be a part of the correct syntax, expressing the output properly:

The use of arrays is easier in Swift, and these arrays will store a collection of data, such as a grid, as a part of a big collection of information. An array called `oddNumbers` will have four figures, such as `(3, 5, 7, 9)`. There will be another array called `songs`, as shown here:

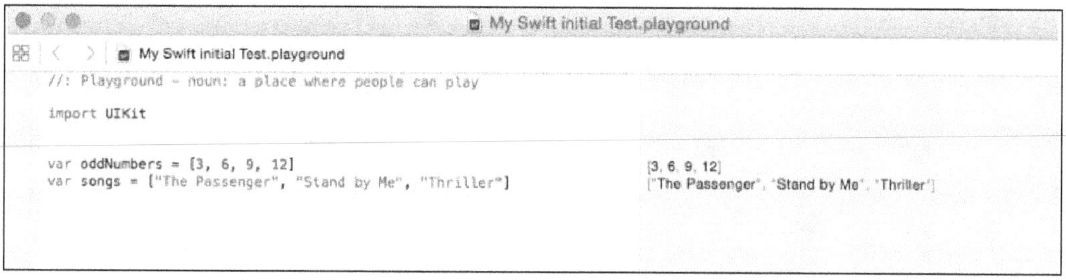

My Swift initial Test.playground
My Swift initial Test.playground
//: Playground - noun: a place where people can play
import UIKit
var oddNumbers = [3, 6, 9, 12]
var songs = ["The Passenger", "Stand by Me", "Thriller"]
[3, 6, 9, 12]
["The Passenger", "Stand by Me", "Thriller"]

The Swift language is vast and has many examples, but we can't cover all of them in this short chapter. This chapter will show you the updates from SQLite, PhoneGap, and some updates on Swift.

For example, the `for` loop is an easier one to use, which is clearly shown in the following screenshot. In this statement, the print statement would have run 10 times as shown in the following screenshot:

My Swift initial Test.playground
My Swift initial Test.playground
//: Playground - noun: a place where people can play
import UIKit
for i in 1...10 {
print("\(i) x 10 is \(i * 10)")
}
(10 times)

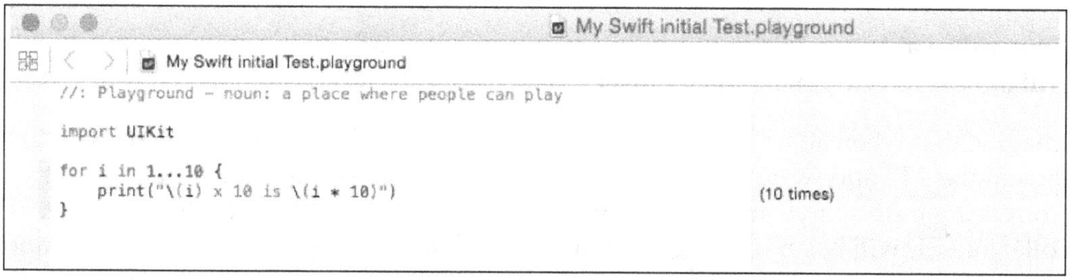

Here is another example of trying to use the `for` command where the number in the loop is not required and _ is used instead. But, the `str` print command has completed its execution five times because the word `gone` was sought, printed, and concatenated, as shown in the following screenshot:

```
//: Playground — noun: a place where people can play

import UIKit
var str = "She is gone"                              "She is gone"

for _ in 1 ... 5 {
    str += " gone"                                   (5 times)
}

print(str)|                                          "She is gone gone gone gone gone gone"
```

As mentioned previously, the use of playgrounds will be — as the name suggests — *Swift and fun to use.*

Just cut and paste it in code and then run it. From Xcode 7 and beyond, the actual code that you can put into playgrounds will be rich, have comments, and be much more than pseudo coding, because it can be added into your apps.

You will be able to add rich text features, comments, and other necessary text that will aid the development and creativity of the programming process.

Imagine that when an update of an API is released, it will be a great and fast way to look at the API and write or hack some code to make it work in playground. Apart from being informative and quick, it will also serve as a training tool for you and your colleagues. It will boost training sessions, and enable developers to try new ideas and programming code without hindrance to others and their common projects.

What a beautifully interactive and modern way to learn and use the existing programming skills to gain new knowledge. The usage and availability of an interactive debugging console in Swift allows a change/enhancement to the product that modernizes its efforts.

Since it was designed from the ground up, Swift aimed to be quick, fast in action and coding, and work with both the Objective-C interoperability and Swift to include and shared libraries, code, and values, as modern 21st century compiler will aid its dominance in the coming years. Objective-C and Swift code can co-exist and work together or separately.

The built-in high performance compiler has been created to maximize the Apple hardware, protocols, and network availability. It is optimized to run very quickly and improve development and compilation speeds.

As part of its portfolio, the Swift language is one of the most modern languages, using the "best of" other scripting languages and removing problems such as poor performance, or syntax related issues to move on from the C and Objective-C code paradigm. There are many languages out there. But Swift is the only one where you can code and learn in a modern way. By learning now, you are preparing for the near future, where this language will be popular. It is a full successor to Objective-C and C-related languages.

Swift has been designed to be modern and opt out of the functionality that would actually stop a programmer developing. So, all the stops for slow development are extinct. For example, all values are, by default, not null. The use of safety for the language has been encouraged and built as part of the software, for example, a variable uses the `var` statement, and the `let` statement will be there for constants. When defining any "Swift" object for example, the value won't be nil because the compiler will deal with it and set it as a part of the safety regime. Enforcing these types of niceties encourages better, professional, cleaner, fun, and innovative code.

Swift has a superbly modern and much-improved error-handling model that will provide a clear and concise way to develop and gain modern skills using state-of-the-art, object-oriented technology. It also captures any necessary error so that the program does not crash, and deal with it. It works nicely with **NSError** and other related iOS frameworks. For example, see the following:

```
func UnloadData() throws { }

func zTest() {
    do {
        try UnloadData()
    } catch {
        print(error)
    }
}
```

Swift2 has now been made open source, which will encourage many more users, on many different platforms, to architect, design, and develop software. It will enable Apple to get into areas of development often used by their competitors in the market place. It will have a huge following, and more so when those faithful Objective-C programmers change to Swift.

New, interesting, and heavy duty code can be written in Swift using some great and powerful language/syntax, with commands such as repeat, defer, and guard. Apple is also providing a migration tool to convert code to new playgrounds and application development code for easy execution. These are some of the benefits that await us for development using Swift2.

Swift is designed to be modern, Swift2 uses information, functionality, and the compiler development from modern research, programming languages, and previous experience of different Apple development, product and coding skills. A modern approach, and the ability to structure extensions and protocols, will ensure that it is around for some time.

Summary

In this chapter, you learned some advanced aspects and future advances of SQLite and how it fits with the current cross-platform development. The chapter outlines the changes of SQLite and its growth and links with PhoneGap. PhoneGap also has integrated with content management systems, such as Adobe Enterprise Manager, which has had several advances in technology, and client license purchases have rocketed its popularity. In this chapter, you have also touched on what is possible in the new Swift language and how it will affect the future of games, apps, and utilities.

Index